INNER JOURNEY

A MEDICAL PERPECTIVE

Edited by
Dr. Peter Mack

With contributions by medical members of the Society for
Medical Advance and Research with Regression Therapy

from the ♡
heart press

Publication by *From the Heart Press:*
First Publication October 2014
Website: www.fromtheheartpress.com

Text copyright: Dr. Peter Mack
ISBN: 978-0-9567887-8-8

A CIP catalogue record for this book is available from the British Library.

Cover Design:
Ashleigh Hanson,
Email: hansonashleigh@hotmail.com

Illustrations:
Wendy Mack,
Email: wendy.mzf@gmail.com

To find out more about the medical therapists contributing to this book, please visit the website: www.smar-rt.com

To contact the editor, Dr. Peter Mack:
Visit the website: www.petermack.sg
Email: dr.pmack@gmail.com

✥✥

"The stories are incredibly inspiring and healing with a powerful impact. I highly recommend this book to those who want to make positive changes in themselves."
Shirley Tay, Holistic Therapist and Teacher

✥✥

"This is a remarkable book on the marvels of regression therapy, written by medical doctors. It offers clear explanations on how regression therapy works by going to the root of the problem, and is vividly illustrated by various case studies. It is a must-read for all healthcare professionals and therapists in holistic healing."
Wendy Yeung, Holistic Therapist

✥✥

CONTRIBUTORS TO THIS BOOK

Dr. Karin Maier-Henle, M.D.

A German physician living in Munich, Karin has undergone specialization in Internal Medicine and Rheumatology. She has a special interest in Alternative Medicine including Homeopathy, Traditional Chinese Medicine and Acupuncture. In addition she has received training in Regression Therapy.

Dr. Moacir Oliveira, M.D.

A Brazilian physician and psychotherapist living in Salvador, Bahia, Moacir has graduated in 1985 and undergone specialization in Psychiatry and Transpersonal Psychology. He has also received training in Regression Therapy under Woolger Training International on Deep Memory Process®.

Dr. Natwar Sharma, M.B.B.S., DNB (Ped), M.R.C.P.C.H. (UK), F.P.C.C. (ISCCM)

A consultant pediatrician living in Chennai, India, Natwar has specialized in pediatric intensive care. He is an assistant professor of Pediatrics in a medical school and Director of Medical Services for an NGO. He has received training in Transpersonal Regression Therapy from the Tasso Institute.

Dr. Peter Mack, M.B.B.S., F.R.C.S.(Ed), F.R.C.S.(Glasg), Ph.D.

A general surgeon living in Singapore, Peter specializes in hepatobiliary and laparoscopic surgery. He has a Doctorate in Medical Science and Master's degrees in Business Administration, Health Economics and Medical Education. He is a Certified Hypnotherapist and has received training in Regression Therapy.

Dr. Sérgio Werner Baumel, M.D.

A Brazilian physician and psychologist living in Vila Velha, Espírito Santo, Sérgio has undergone specialization in Clinical Neurology, Intensive Care Medicine and Sexology. He is taking his Master's degree in Social Psychology. He has also received training in Ericksonian Hypnotherapy and Regression Therapy.

Dr. Soumya Rao P., M.B.B.S., M.R.C.Psych.

An Indian psychiatrist living in Bangalore, India, Soumya has attended medical school in Bangalore and pursued her postgraduate training in Psychiatry in the United Kingdom. She is a Certified Regression Therapist from the Life Research Academy in Hyderabad, India.

CONTENTS

DISCLAIMER

The information provided in this book is designed to provide helpful information on the subjects discussed. The ideas and advice in the book are opinions of the authors themselves and given in their personal capacity. While many of the clinical vignettes describe dramatic and transformational outcomes, it is not the intention of the authors to sensationalize regression hypnotherapy. Rather, the purpose is to create a wider awareness of an underutilized method of treatment. No claims are made of any miraculous effectiveness. No therapists should use the powerful techniques of regression therapy unless they are adequately trained in them. The patient's suitability for regression therapy must be individualized on the basis of his symptoms, pathology, emotional makeup and belief system. The names and identities of the people in the stories have been changed to protect their confidentiality, while preserving the spirit of the work. References are provided for informational purposes only and do not constitute endorsement of any sources.

FOREWORD

The development of the human race has numerous examples of people who have stood up against a prevailing culture with new ideas and thoughts. There was a time when cultures believed the sun went round the earth. Yet when Galileo stood up and said the earth went round the sun he was threatened with heresy by an inquisition and imprisoned. When sailing ships started to explore the oceans the culture at the time said they would fall off the end of the earth. Yet when those early pioneers came back their stories changed peoples thinking. Of course all these changes did not happen overnight, and when the pioneers stood up against fear and threats it called for great bravery. If they had not do so we would still think the earth was flat and the sun went around the earth.

Turning to the medical world, this has made enormous advances in surgery, anesthetics and in vaccines to prevent illness. But in terms of understanding who we really are, understanding why illness happens and the causes of disease, it is almost as if it has made no progress at all.

Some of the early medical doctors who stood up with new ideas about this, like Dr. Brian Weiss, had to go through fear and rejection just like the early pioneers. He had to leave his job as a psychiatrist because he talked about past lives and its affect on our health. But he stood firm and wrote his books that have touched hundreds of thousands of people. There are other medical doctors standing up with their views. Dr. Newton Kondaveti and his wife Dr. Lakshmi G.V. in India are training medical doctors to work with past lives and have a program to take this work to every hospital in India.

So this book is a step in starting to bring to the Western world awareness of how regression therapy, which includes past life regression, can be used by medical doctors to bring about transformational changes. And in some cases after just a few sessions it may seem like miracle work. This is not an alternative to the amazing medical practices that exist in the West. It is a complementary approach that will take medicine into a new paradigm.

We have already seen how the use of meditation can reduce people's stress and help improve healing speed, and how this has been incorporated into the medical model. Of course it took research and proof, but research can take many forms. There still is a need for the more traditional form of research, which is what the *Society of Advance and Research with Regression Therapy* will be doing. But hopefully this book will bring an awareness of the possibilities before that research is completed.

The pioneers who founded America did not have to wait for Columbus to sail to America a hundred times. They sent out their ships and explored as soon as they heard the news; they were of course careful on those journeys but this sped up the development of America as we know it today.

So whenever a new idea comes that makes logical sense and feels intuitively right, then others can follow. And when we look back in a hundred years' time we will wonder why these changes did not happen faster. Imagine living in a world where emotionally based disease and illness can be resolved without pharmaceuticals and their side effects. Imagine a world where people can completely transform their problems rather than just reduce their symptoms. Think of the millions who suffer depression and anxiety, obsessions, disharmony and the turmoil in business and in the home. Think of the change that can be done, and how the medical profession holds the key to unlock all of this. This is a tool that is presented to them by the brave medical doctors in this book who are prepared to share their stories and their successes. Without them, and all the other brave people throughout history who have brought about change, we would not be where we are now.

If the reader has doubts about some of these approaches and procedures, all they are asked to do is to have an open mind and know that the honesty and integrity of these doctors is intact. These are their stories and successes, and it is possible to grow this work rapidly around the world.

It is about tapping into the very core of what the medical world calls the "placebo effect" – this unknown, this sudden healing that takes place and gets in the way of pharmaceutical trials. We are actually harnessing people's ability to heal themselves. To do this we have to treat the person as a whole – a physical part, an emotional part, a mental part and a spiritual part. You cannot work with just one part in isolation.

Of course this approach is not a panacea to resolve all people's problems at any time. When we understand that illness and disease is there for a purpose and has a message, then the timing has to be right to have the desired effect. And when the time is not right we need to respect that each person has a different path and a different way of growing through their challenges.

The first step to healing is for the person to want to change and know what caused the problem in the first place. Then the energetic blockage that is stopping change needs to be cleared. When people connect with their feeling heart they are able to think and act differently and bring this into their current life in a meaningful way. This is what regression therapy does as a complete process. Of course people can find lots of ways to heal themselves simply by living their lives and working through their fear and difficulties. But this is a tool that speeds up this healing process and enables people to bring about meaningful changes quicker and in a more harmonious way whilst respecting their individual need.

It certainly does not claim to be a religion, and it does not claim to be a replacement for medical procedures. It is a complementary approach, and for more people in the future it will be their preferred choice.

Andy Tomlinson
October 2014

PREFACE

In April 2013, fourteen physicians and five psychologists from six countries met in Porto, Portugal, to form the *Society for Medical Advance and Research with Regression Therapy* (SMAR-RT). The group's aim was to discuss ways of conducting research in regression therapy and promoting awareness of this underutilized form of psychotherapy to the wider medical community. Arising out of this discussion, a decision was made to put in writing some our members' personal experience, in story form, for sharing with a wider readership.

"Share your knowledge. It is a way to achieve immortality."
Dalai Lama XIV

This book is the outcome of the collective effort of this international group. The members share a common belief that all patients have an intrinsic core of self-healing capability, which when appropriately unleashed and harnessed can initiate a process of rapid healing within them. Hence the phrase "Inner Healing Journey" is adopted as the title for this book.

As in all other medical disciplines, the progressive and eventual acceptance of regression therapy is expected to rest on a strong evidence base. What perhaps is less obvious, at this point in time, is the nature and form of the desired evidence. In conventional medicine, healthcare professionals are accustomed to the use of the randomized controlled clinical trial as the gold standard for evaluating drug efficacy. Inevitably, they tend to be inclined to view the value of all research activities from that perspective, and expect our group to conduct research along similar lines. However, at the heart of the emotional symptoms and psychosocial issues that regression therapists normally deal with are complex phenomena that lead to healing outcomes of a non-random nature. As such, the evidence that would be most suitable for advancing the quality of regression work is necessarily qualitative rather than quantitative. It can be inferred, therefore, that the mainstay of our investigative methodology would consist not of randomized trials, but of narrative analysis and case studies.

Case studies are story-like anecdotes, and stories in themselves are powerful tools for healing. Just as knowledge can evolve into wisdom, so can facts evolve into a story. When a therapist decides to awaken the patient's sleeping wisdom through a story rather than to convince the patient of a perspective through facts, a subtle but powerful shift occurs. The patient learns to make a wise rather than a "right" decision. This is because a good story helps the patient to find new meaning, and influences the interpretation he gives to the facts before him. After all, facts stay neutral and have little impact until people add their own meaning to them. The value that regression therapy brings to the healing process resides in its ability to help to add meaning to facts pertinent to the patient through appropriately retrieved stories of his past.

Several of our members have documented their experiences in regression therapy as narratives in this book. All patient names are pseudonyms, to protect their identities. Two main categories of narratives have been included. The first category consists of stories of an emotional nature, and involving relationship issues. The second category pertains to those medical illnesses that are unresolved by traditional treatment. Intriguingly, these patient stories, though coming from different cultures and geographical zones, portray a consistent healing pattern.

Authors from various parts of Asia, Europe, and South America have contributed eleven patient stories. I have written the first two chapters in Part One myself, covering the therapy process of a middle-aged lady who has struggled through the emotional turmoil of her marriage crisis. The two chapters represent the two phases of her inner healing journey. Sufficient details of the regression technique and process have been included to take the myth out of the therapy.

Part Two is on "Love and Relationships" and has three stories with backgrounds from three different countries. In Chapter 3, Dr. Soumya Rao P. from India shares her understanding of how inner child healing can be incorporated into regression therapy. In Chapter 4, Dr. Karin Maier-Henle from Germany highlights the importance of self-love, and how the lack of it generates emotional handicaps in living. In Chapter 5, Dr. Sérgio Werner Baumel from Brazil shares his trials and tribulations in treating a patient with an impaired ability to express love, over several years.

The last four chapters in Part Three deal with the use of regression therapy in various medical conditions. In Chapters 6 and 7, Dr. Moacir Oliveira illustrates how body psychotherapy, psychodrama and past life therapy can be integrated to effectively to treat refractory asthma and fibromyalgia. In Chapter 8, Dr. Natwar Sharma relates his experience in the use of metaphoric narratives for healing in autoimmune disorders. Dr. Sérgio has kindly volunteered to end the book in Chapter 9 with two unique examples of how he attempts to use regression as an aid to enhance fertility.

I like to thank all contributors for having given their time and energy in sharing their crown jewels in this book, and all our patients who have graciously allowed their stories to be shared. Their dedication to promoting the art and practice of regression

7

has been invaluable. In particular, Andy Tomlinson has been instrumental in initiating the formation of SMAR-RT and providing the driving force and moral support behind the production of this book. I would also like to thank Shirley Tay and Wendy Yeung, my therapist colleagues who have helped to read the manuscript and offered their valuable comments.

Dr. Peter Mack
October 2014

INTRODUCTION

Perspectives in Healing

Dr. Peter Mack

"Scars have the strange power to remind us that our past is real."

Cormac McCarthy
In: All the Pretty Horses, 1992

The practice of regression therapy rests on a paradigm that is different from that of conventional medicine. As medical professionals, we are attuned to look at disease as an organ-system malfunction that is correctible by restoring physiological homeostasis through some form of medical intervention. In contrast, as regression therapists, we adopt the view that beneath all the illness and problems of our lives is an "inner essence" within us that can heal. This essence consists of a consciousness that carries the qualities of love, compassion and wisdom, the power of which can be unleashed through the processing of our buried memories. Beneath our concealing masks are sublimated thoughts and damaged emotions lurking in our subconscious mind that affect our view of life and our relationships. Once we recognize and remember who we are at our core, healing begins.

Conventional medical thinking regards healing as the restoration of a physical state or condition. Common examples of

9

healing in medicine are: the union of a fractured bone, reduction in pain level, decrease in tumor burden or the normalization of an elevated blood sugar level. In regression therapy however, healing assumes a much broader meaning. It is about perfecting what is imperfect. Over and above the introduction of physical changes, it may include the eradication of an undesirable habit, letting go of a desire, a shift in an emotional state or a change in perception and attitude.

It is important to distinguish a "disease" from an "illness". An illness is what the patient has, whereas a disease is the diagnosis given to him by the doctor. Stated differently, an illness is viewed not through the diagnostic lens of symptoms, physical signs and medical investigations, but as a life challenge in itself. The illness that befalls a patient is inextricably bound up with the phenomenon of meaning. In fact, everything that happens to us, including all sicknesses, events and relationships, has a meaning. An illness changes the patient through its inherent meaning and affects the individual's thoughts, actions, behavior and response to the people around him. Through experiencing the suffering associated with the illness, the patient is able to reach inside himself and discover his greatest qualities of strength, power and will that can help him evolve to his next level of growth.

The idea of healing is also broader in scope than the concept of curing. Apart from the correction of physiological imbalance, healing implies an achievement of personal wholesomeness. The dimensions of wholesomeness can include the capacity for insight, love, intimacy, understanding, compassion and soul growth. In other words, healing can be "transformational" in addition to being "restorative" in correcting a disorder or illness. It can also be "transpersonal" as well as "personal" in the nature of personal change that results. It embraces the dual concepts of "regeneration" and "recovery" at both the physical and emotional levels.

With this perspective, emotional wounds and suffering in illnesses are deemed to be of value to the patient. In a sense, they provide opportunities for the individual to savor the lessons and discover the purpose of the wound. For instance, many of us may fall ill and encounter hardships at some point in our lives, but may be unaware of our own courage. As such, we may be at a loss on how to overcome our life challenges until we reach the limits of our emotional strength. More often than not, we choose to quickly retreat from the suffering with the assumption that avoidance protects us from the associated pain. Unfortunately, our focus on avoiding and eliminating suffering in our lives perpetuates and potentiates our fear of living.

"When things fall apart, consider the possibility that life knocked it down on purpose. Not to bully you, or to punish you, but to prompt you to build something that better suits your personality and your purpose. Sometimes things fall apart so that better things can fall together."

Sandra King

All wounds have a history, and memories of our history reside in the depths of our subconscious mind. We are often hurt and bewildered by the ambiguities of love and conflict in our lives. Early in our childhood, many of us may have been neglected or emotionally abused by our parents or caretakers. When the abuse has been internalized, we may manifest withdrawal and depression. Sometimes we may even become haunted by feelings of low self-esteem, loneliness, rejection and resignation. When we grow up and commit ourselves to a career, a relationship or a marriage, the meaning of our lives is automatically invested in these feelings. Despite our best efforts, the structure of our relationships can fall apart and the crisis of meaning can become profound. In such situations, regression therapy enables us to get to the origin of our wounds. Our awakening to the pain brings an opportunity to heal and grow, in times of crisis. This becomes a critical time of change in the lives of many people, and the change process is always related to the idea of "making whole again".

A medical colleague, who has been quietly studying my work, surprised me one day by describing regression therapy as a form of "healing through story-telling." I agreed. Stories heal, and they heal all the more effectively if the story-telling is done under hypnosis. In fact, past life stories elicited by regression have a reputation for their power to heal obscure and unexplained symptoms. As the readers will soon realize, stories can also be reworked and reframed, from time to time, during therapy. This gives the patient the choice of deciding how he wants his personal story to end in order to meet his healing needs.

The stories told in this book revolve around the use of regression therapy for learning life lessons, which in turn open our hearts to transformational healing. Sufficient procedural detail has been included in some of the case studies to enable the readers to grasp the essence of the regression process. The stories are written to show how the therapy helps the patients, and the manner in which the unavoidable mysteries of pain and suffering in their lives can give rise to hidden resources of compassion and creativity. From these anecdotes, the reader will get a feel of how some determined individuals have been able to grapple with their life challenges and succeed in translating their emotional struggles into meaningful discovery processes.

PART ONE

Marriage Crisis

CHAPTER ONE

Marriage Crisis I: Healing Journey

Dr. Peter Mack

"We learn through our relationships, which present opportunities for giving and receiving love and for practicing patience, compassion and charity. They are also tests, supplying us with feedback on whether or not we are learning these and other lessons. Are we patient and loving with each other, or are we fearful and frustrated? Our relationships provide the answers and point the way to spiritual growth."

Dr. Brian Weiss, MD
In: Miracles Happen, 2012

My first encounter with regression hypnotherapy dates back to my undergraduate days when I witnessed a clinical demonstration during an evening seminar delivered by a British dental surgeon. At that time there was budding interest in the use of hypnosis for dental and medical anesthesia, but unfortunately it was short-lived. The enthusiasm faded so rapidly that it never reached the stage where it was considered for application to psychotherapy.

After completing medical school, I specialized in surgery, developed an active interest in medical research and obtained my Doctorate in Medical Science. Next, I went through a revolutionary era in which the practice of medicine rapidly changed with remarkable advances in medical technology, drugs and imaging techniques. However, I remained consciously aware of the presence of a significant number of patients with unexplained symptoms for which no physiological basis could be ascribed, and I felt disturbed by it. Deep within, I sensed that additional tools were needed for my healing armamentarium.

My Journey as Therapist

Decades later, I re-ignited my youthful dream of learning hypnosis, and underwent formal training in both conventional hypnotherapy and regression therapy. Since then, as I apply these techniques to my patients, I have witnessed to my amazement frequent instances of dramatic healing, which I had hardly ever come across previously. So I decided to pursue my interest in this particular mode of psychotherapy.

At this point, a unique patient came into my life. She was a young lady in her mid-twenties and was suffering from repeated attacks of syncope and plagued by a myriad of associated symptoms including insomnia, anxiety, mood changes, auditory hallucinations and amnesia. It soon became obvious to me that she was struggling with severe emotional trauma and was "stuck" in her life, despite medical treatment. After an intensive course of regression therapy over eighteen days, she astonished me with a transformational change. From that moment onwards my view of regression therapy has never been the same again. At her request, her story has since been published in the book *Healing Deep Hurt Within*.

Since then, I have explored the use of the techniques of regression hypnotherapy in a variety of clinical problems, particularly those with unexplained medical symptoms. The amazing experience is that I have often been rewarded with encouraging and dramatic clinical outcomes.

In the following section, I am sharing the story of a middle-aged lady who was emotionally downtrodden with an ailing marriage relationship and devastated by her crisis. She sensed herself drifting towards the verge of depression and was looking desperately for professional help. After completing her treatment, she realized to her own enlightenment that her healing outcome had not been merely a corrective experience in behavior and cognition, but one that was transformational in mind and spirit.

THE CASE OF CINDY – CRUMBLING MARRIAGE

Relationships can become very turbulent between couples at times, but the key to managing a marriage crisis lies with understanding why the relationship fails in the first place. To start with, making meaning out of the marriage contract is a significant challenge in modern life. As an idealized concept, marriage breeds an expectation of stability and permanence, but unfortunately such a concept is potentially in conflict with one's search for meaning in life.

Life is a process that involves constant change, and this forms a stark contrast to the stability of meaning. When the act of marriage imposes its constancy of meaning onto life's changing state, a dilemma begins. Frequently, when a married couple becomes busy highlighting each other's deficiencies instead of enjoying each other's company, they begin to realize that their married lives are structured according to enduring precepts that do not correspond to how they expect life should naturally flow. Yet their matrimonial vows, marital commitments and legal constraints do not embrace the expectation of a divorce. When this happens, a crisis begins to loom.

A message flashed onto my computer monitor one Sunday morning as I opened my mailbox. The sender has signed herself off as Cindy, and the first sentence immediately caught my attention.

"Dr. Mack, I am currently facing the most difficult phase of my 40 years of life and I am looking for some help."

It was dated as 4:00 am, 30 September 2012, and conveyed a clear sense of urgency. In fact it seemed to be raising an alarm, and I felt compelled to read on.

"My relationship with my husband has not been well since the start of our marriage. I am now at a critical point when a decision needs to be made – whether to break or keep working at it. This past year has been particularly challenging for my personal growth. I have managed to rediscover myself and feel the change in me. I am also calmer and feeling lighter. These good feelings continue to grow as I discover the literature on past life regression therapy and spirituality. However, as a result of my marriage life I have become depressed over the past year.

As I am regaining my old self, my marriage problems have remained unchanged. I am preoccupied with a lot of reading, sorting out my thoughts and finding my purpose of life. Whilst I have come to accept my life as it is, suddenly on last Friday, I discovered that my husband is giving up on our marriage. He no longer accepts our differences. I am feeling suffocated with chest pain and insecurity. It feels as if a bomb has just exploded on me and all the negative feelings have returned. By 16 October 2012 we will have been married for nine years, and this is a long time. A part of me is telling me to be strong and keep going but another part of me is saying that the end has come. I have been contemplating past life regression therapy to seek answers for myself. Will you help me please?"

It was a well thought-out message and the sender struck me as being emotionally desperate, yet sufficiently insightful and determined to take charge of her own crisis. I pondered over her mail for some time and finally decided to meet up with her.

It was on the following Tuesday at 12:15 pm when I stepped into the hospital café at the ground floor. A soft, clear voice came from one corner of the cafe and immediately caught my attention.

"Dr. Mack, I am Cindy." An elegant lady of medium height politely stood up to introduce herself. A pair of dark brown eyes was glinting in my direction. Unmistakably I sensed her desperate need for help.

Cindy had thin eyebrows with short, sparse eyelashes that were devoid of mascara. Her wavy, shoulder-length hair was brunette in color. What was obvious was her broad-based nose and thin lips with a prominent chin. She greeted me with a wide smile but her weary complexion gave away the clue that she had been struggling with sleepless nights of late. She was actively holding back her tears while fighting to be strong. After struggling for a minute she was unable to initiate a conversation. Her eyes welled up and I sensed that her pain was overflowing. I whispered to her softly, "It's okay to let go."

Somehow, Cindy felt a little embarrassed. She sniffed, wiped her tears and regained her composure. Then she confessed that she had prepared a script beforehand so that she could communicate her issues more coherently.

"No problem," I said, appreciating the effort she had put in. "Just begin when you are ready." She nodded thankfully and a story flowed.

Cindy grew up in a well-to-do Chinese family with one sister and three elder brothers, all of whom were very successful businessmen. Her father had passed away when she was seventeen. She migrated from Indonesia to Singapore about fourteen years ago and worked in the financial sector. Subsequently she met Kent, her current husband, through the Social Development Unit. This was a governmental body that was created three decades ago to foster opportunities for singles to interact in social settings.

Kent, on the other hand, came from a lower middle-income group and had experienced an unhappy childhood. He had earlier struggled with his school studies, and currently with his career development. In contrast, his brother was a government scholar and excelled in his career performance. Kent had failed to get into a good school, and after growing up he had been blaming his slow career growth on his educational background. Although he loved business development, his mother believed that he was probably better off with a salaried, deskbound and nine-to-five job. At one stage his father was jobless; the family finances were tight and he was under tremendous stress.

Cindy and Kent were quickly attracted to each other but experienced frequent disagreements over a variety of issues. Despite their quarrels, their relationship stayed intact and they got married after eight months of courtship. They went through an extremely grand wedding ceremony in Jakarta attended by 1,500 guests. Many of these guests were prominent business leaders and Kent was emotionally overwhelmed. The event was followed immediately by a second wedding banquet in Singapore and the family members on both sides were exceedingly proud.

Amidst the high expectations, the wedding night was a letdown. Kent avoided sexual intimacy that evening and Cindy was dismayed and disappointed. She never learned the precise reason for his behavior and had difficulty forgiving him since. Shortly afterwards, Kent's problem of erectile dysfunction became clinically manifest. It was tough for Cindy to accept. She tried all ways to help. She read around the subject matter, actively encouraged him to relax, but her efforts failed to help.

Several weeks later, the marriage was consummated after some struggle. Unfortunately, the occasion brought pain instead of joy. Kent had rushed through the act before Cindy was ready and her external genitalia were torn during the forceful penetration. She bled as a result. Accompanied by her sister, Cindy visited her gynecologist the next day, while Kent was shying away in the background and guilt-laden.

At one stage, Kent was able to relax better, while he also resorted to medication as an aid. As things went along, Cindy learned how to blend in and the quality of their sexual intimacy improved. It wasn't regular though, and by then Cindy had resigned herself to the fact that she had always to be the one to initiate it.

In the meantime, day-to-day conflicts continued. While Cindy perceived spousal disagreements as healthy intellectual exchanges, Kent felt them as an unfair assault on his masculine ego. In the interest of harmony, he stayed passive and gave way to her domineering views. Kent's paradigm had always been that the man should be the provider for the family, and his level of performance reinforced Cindy's perception that he had failed to live up to his expectations of himself. The angst was sunk inside him and started to erode into his self-esteem. "It is something that he has to work out for himself and I do not know how to help," Cindy remarked.

Time passed and Cindy became pregnant. However, the imminent arrival of their first child brought little joy to the family. She was alone at home most of the time and did not receive the love and care she expected from her husband. Coping with morning sickness and the weight of the enlarging abdomen made her feel down. Kent had never, for a moment, consoled her nor bothered to ask what she would like for her meals. He even absented himself at the time of her delivery because he felt uncomfortable with the agony of her labor pains.

The first child was a boy, and Kent was not attached to him. Cindy was disappointed. A few years later, they had a baby girl. This time the birth experience was better. Nonetheless, Kent continued to spend little time with either child. The marriage relationship continued to deteriorate and Cindy sensed herself sliding into depression. With few friends to turn to in her difficult moments, she struggled to manage her moods. As their marriage difficulties heightened with frequent quarrels, Cindy initiated arrangements for marriage counseling. Kent went with her initially, but reluctantly. His efforts didn't last. When the counselor touched on the issue of intimacy, Kent's sensitivity heightened and he stopped attending the counseling sessions altogether.

Kent worked as a real estate agent with his own team of staff and was aiming to be the branch manager of his company. He recently won a top sales award from his company but his superiors blocked him from receiving the honor publicly. Upset with the corporate backstabbing, he threw in the towel and found himself a new job. With the change of company, there was a transition period during which he faced cash-flow problems. He asked Cindy for unconditional support. After evaluating his proposal with her usual financial prowess, she concluded his plan was unsound. Unfortunately, she did not foresee that her turning down his request was the last straw for their marriage.

A week ago, Kent suddenly divulged his intention to divorce Cindy. Shocked and dumbfounded, she could not understand how things could have become that awry.

"I really don't wish my marriage to be over like that, but it's too late now," Cindy said remorsefully. "I feel so sorry and regretful that I wasn't aware of Kent's feeling. He says he is feeling trapped and empty and is at his rock bottom now. He can't feel for me anymore. He is very frustrated, angry and lonely. It seems our marriage relationship is on the path of no return. The torment of emotional pain is killing me inside and I need to get my life back."

The emotional turmoil had taken a toll on Cindy's health. Physical symptoms appeared. She felt tight in her chest and gastric spasms kept her awake at night. Over the past week she had experienced an unbearable aching sensation at the back of her neck for which she had sought acupuncture treatment.

"I didn't know the criticality of the situation," Cindy sobbed. "His decision made me depressed and I couldn't accept it. In fact he was very surprised that I received the news so badly."

"So he thought that you were aware of his emotional and mental state all along?" I asked.

"Yes," she paused. "And I must say I have been the bad person because I kept challenging him in all his ideas and decisions. I did not know what I did was hurting because he had never responded to my arguments. Or maybe he did but I failed to detect the subtleness of his counterarguments. In hindsight I shouldn't have done a lot of things, but it is too late."

It was a wake-up call. Cindy badly wanted to find a way to make sense of this event because she believed she might still be able to reverse the situation.

"I think a lot of stress has been accumulated from Kent's childhood. I remember detecting his inner turmoil at one stage after our marriage. I have talked to him about it before. I notice the way he treats me is identical to the way he treats his parents. He seems to have some self-awareness and is frustrated with what he is, but not willing to face the reality."

It was a long conversation. Cindy's issue sounded complex and I wondered how I could possibly help. As a therapist, I had learned not to regard her, the patient, as the problem but her problem itself as the problem. It suddenly occurred to me to ask her, "But ... what do you expect to get out of past life therapy?"

"I don't dare to expect anything," she replied frankly. "My life has been quite blissful in the past, but marriage difficulties bother me. I can feel that my husband and I are both working very hard in the relationship. Yet, there is a block between us and I want to know what that is. I am grappling with the fact that my marriage is over. The hardest part is to face the truth and go through it. I am also concerned about my children, as I don't want my constant emotional instability to affect their psychological and mental growth. I need help to stabilize my mind in going forward. I am prepared to accept what the universe has planned for me. I still do not know what is the lesson I am supposed to learn, but trust me: I do not want to come back another lifetime to re-learn my lesson!"

An hour and half passed. Cindy's mood had lightened up in the course of our conversation. I was impressed with her clarity of purpose, and decided that I would try to help her. However, I set the condition that she must resume her daily meditation practice that she had discontinued for many years.

Meditation is a deliberate effort undertaken by an individual to come to a contemplative experience of reality and bliss through the power of the mind. Cindy seemed to understand the process and phenomenon quite well. I explained to her that once she had control over her mind she would become less disturbed by her failures. Meditation, being a personal creative process, could be customized to her own temperament and help her to get a handle on her self-concept.

At home that evening, Cindy experienced a significant improvement in her wellbeing. Her chest tightness diminished significantly and she slept better. "There was a feeling of myself drawn towards clarity," she said. "I woke up in the morning feeling a little zest and went on to do some stretching exercise in the gym. This was not something I usually do! I am extremely grateful and blessed that in a time like this I am given someone to pull me up. Your commitment and willingness has impressed me tremendously and it continues to spur me up."

Session 1: Archetypal Scenes of Self

After a week of daily meditation exercises, Cindy improved emotionally and was looking forward to starting her therapy. It was the afternoon of 9 October 2012. Dressed in a smart white, long-sleeved shirt and gray pants, she turned up in good spirits in my clinic.

Being her first exposure to hypnotherapy, I induced her slowly into a trance state. After a short breathing exercise and a progressive muscular relaxation, she went into moderately deep trance. An emotion emerged spontaneously.

"I feel sad," she said, and started sobbing. "I need more space in my heart. It's too tight ... I need more room ... I want more freedom."

The use of the word "freedom" puzzled me initially.

Nine years ago, Cindy's mother had been critically ill and she was under strong family pressure to get married. At that time she was unsure if Kent was her appropriate life partner, but in the

25

heat of the situation she decided in his favor. Soon after the marriage, her dominating character prompted her to shape him the way she wanted rather than letting him be himself. Kent described their marriage relationship as being characterized by "a hundred per cent disagreement." On Cindy's part, she felt she had sacrificed her personal interests and hobbies after her marriage to focus on her daily family routines. She had neglected her social life in the process, and therefore felt emotionally trapped with a sense of lack of freedom.

With Cindy under hypnosis, I prompted her to focus on her thought of her "need for freedom." The technique worked, and a series of archetypal imagery emerged spontaneously.

First, Cindy saw herself as a ten-year-old girl, alone and enjoying herself in a meadow. Feeling happy and carefree, she was holding a stick and playing in a paddy field. Her feelings of "being trapped" suddenly escalated as she saw herself in this carefree state. This quest for freedom was something that she had unconsciously been longing for.

Next, Cindy drifted on to another scene. She was initially perplexed when she visualized herself as a man, the head of a household, returning home after a hard day's work. The wife and son were attending to him with respect while dinner was being served. Soon it became clear that this imagery was archetypal of her late father's life struggles.

Then a third archetypal scene emerged. The imagery of this scene turned out to be very significant in terms of meaning and healing.

"I see myself alone at the seaside. I am a grown-up woman in my twenties. I like to hear the sound of the waves. I am alone and the feel of the sand is very smooth. I feel very peaceful ... and am reflecting over various things in my life. I am sitting, staring at the sea and hearing the sound of the waves. I feel very lonely. Then I walk home to cook my dinner and watch television.

The house is very modern, like in a Western country, and is overlooking the sea. I am occupying the house alone. It's evening time. I take out some food from the fridge and start cooking. I turn on the television and watch the program as I eat my meal. Well, this is also what I do in my current life. Oh, my mind is floating ..."

After the session, Cindy was impressed with her own hypnotizability. The image of her solitary self at the beach echoed her current feeling of loneliness. As all her subsequent therapy sessions eventually showed, the seaside imagery was a consistent component of her healing experience.

Session 2: Hypnodrama

Encouraged by the outcome of her first session, Cindy returned eagerly the next day. This time, however, I used an affect bridge and the therapy session took on a different slant.

As I directed Cindy to focus on her relationship with her spouse, a desperate emotion emerged. "I feel helpless. There is pain and tightness in the chest." Cindy started to sob. "I am surrendering ... I am scared of whatever is coming ... I do not know whether I have the ability to face it ... I see darkness."

Cindy burst into tears, but I prompted her to continue.

"I feel very lonely. I see myself sitting alone inside a dark room. A light is shining on me. I am in deep thought, and am thinking and searching for a solution. I am in a daze ... I couldn't find a way out. I am sitting on a chair in front of a table. My palms are on my face. There is an electrical light shining from the ceiling. I am thinking hard."

"What is the problem you are trying to solve?" I asked.

"How do I make things better? I have a lot of questions that I have no answers to. How am I going to come out of this situation? How should I move forward? What will happen next? Which road should I choose? ... I am stuck," she said with a trembling voice.

Next, Cindy visualized herself walking out of the room to stroll by the beach, and she was in a scene identical to what she had experienced the day before. She was enjoying the sight and

28

sound of the sea waves and the feel of the breeze. She sat down to reflect on her life. Suddenly she spoke her thoughts aloud.

"Things don't have to be this way! I am so close but he (Kent) is so far. I keep thinking ... how do I make him understand? My husband has the capability. I see the greatness in him, but he has used it in the wrong way. He can't let go of the past and I find him pitiful ... pitiful for someone who has so much greatness but yet cannot see. He doesn't realize what he is doing to himself. I do not know how to help him ... I am lost ... I cannot decide. If I let go, I don't know what is going to happen next. If I do not let go, it causes suffering because I am not confident that he will connect with the children. What should I do?"

Pain was mounting. I sensed Cindy was trying to figure out an alternative form of action that could be executed if she had a second chance in the marriage relationship. Intuitively I felt the use of hypnodrama was appropriate at this point.

Hypnodrama is the hypnotic version of psychodrama[1]. Its use in regression therapy would enable me to access Cindy's and her husband's consciousness alongside each other. The subsequent interaction between them would create an opportunity for her story to be reframed. It would also help her to discover her deeper feelings and bring her preconscious attitudes and beliefs to the surface.

"Visualize the image of your husband standing in front of you," I prompted.

Kent's image appeared instantly and Cindy went into a strong catharsis. Somehow, the emergence of her husband's image carried enormous transformational power.

---

[1] Psychodrama is an action technique in psychotherapy that involves the use of role playing and dramatic self-presentation for the patient to gain insight into his life.

"Ask him how he feels about his own situation right now," I asked.

"He says, *I am lost*," Cindy said.

"Ask in what way you can help him."

"He says, *I don't need your help. I just want to be left alone. I will prove that I can make it*."

"Tell him how you feel about his situation from the bottom of your heart." I intentionally guided Cindy to phrase her comments as direct statements to her husband, so as to focus her consciousness on the here and now with a sharper degree of awareness.

"I love you," she said to Kent, crying aloud and explosively.

A minute passed. I understood that, by allowing Cindy to express her feelings aloud, it would make her experience more vivid and enhance the healing process. Crying away, Cindy said: "It is difficult for me to see him in that state."

"Look at Kent in his eyes. Did he hear what you just said?"

"Yes. He says, *I am not worthy of your love*. I ask him why he feels that way when I am doing everything for him, but he doesn't have an answer. He says, *I don't want to be like that too*. (crying) He says he has had enough of trying for nine years and that it's time we go separate ways. I ask him why he must leave me after nine years. He replies that he doesn't have any more feelings for me. I am a stranger to him now."

It was a difficult moment. I felt privileged that Cindy had confided in me with her free expression of emotions. With her continual cathartic release of pent-up tension during the therapy session, I expected her healing to be prompt. Unknowingly, she had slid into a deep trance that helped her to interact with Kent's consciousness to discover new beliefs and possibilities for changing her life.

The underlying principle of hypnodrama is that of combining visualization and improvisation. Applying this principle would require Cindy to refocus herself as if things were happening in the here and now.

"Ask him how you can be less of a stranger to him."

"He is quiet ... He tells me that I won't be able to change anything because we are not meant for each other and cannot understand each other."

"Ask him what you must do to understand him better."

There was a pause.

Suddenly, Cindy burst into tears again as the deep inner silence was broken through a solemn communication. "He still cares," she said as she was crying away. The primary occupation of Cindy's conscious mind had been bypassed and impositions from the past were being suspended.

"He tries to block his feelings from me ... he breaks down ... he feels helpless. He asks me to leave him alone. He wants to handle everything by himself and in his own way."

"Tell him that you respect his wishes and that you want to help him to handle it better, even if it is in his own way."

There was another pause.

"He calms down now and feels better."

"Give him a hug and you will be able to sense his feelings better now." I suggested making a gesture of love as I passed her a pillow. The gesture would add vividness and ownership to Cindy's experience.

"I sense pain. Oh! He loves me too ..." Cindy cried again and much louder this time. I waited. It took another minute before the intense catharsis settled down.

"I want you to visualize yourself, in a moment, to be in a special and safe place. It is a place of comfort with peace and healing. Let yourself enjoy the sights and sounds in this place, captivated by all the possibilities and all that you both can experience …"

"We are facing the sea now." Cindy instantly calmed down.

I decided to ride on her selected mental imagery and move her forward with a healing script.

"Look at the sea and listen to the roaring waves. With every wave coming to the shore, let it wash away your pain, frustration and sorrow. With each succeeding wave you feel increasingly lighter in your heart. You walk along the beach and allow the seawater to splash onto your feet and cleanse your hurt. Soon the healing sinks into your body and the two of you feel increasingly closer to each other. This is the moment you are united with your husband, with or without the need for words. It is all one heart and mind and you feel the unconditional love in each other."

The session ended with an air of astonishment. Cindy was surprised she could still feel Kent's love for her. Their quarrels throughout the years had led her to believe that their love was dead. However, her hope had just been re-ignited. She was re-believing in what had suddenly convinced her to be the truth. The guided imagery had separated her from her old way of thinking and behaving. It was also the power of now that provided the space where new choices were made possible. Enriched by new possibilities of thought, Cindy had suddenly become unstuck. She now appreciated the meaning of unconditional love. As we integrated her experience in our subsequent dialogue, she was filled with insights.

"Kent has a lot of grudge in him and against his parents, relatives and friends. It is as if everybody owes him a living. I know his problem but can't help him to solve it. How can he live his life with baggage in this manner? It is very tiring. In the process I have been swirled in and acquired more and more baggage myself. Maybe this is why I talked about freedom in my therapy session yesterday. It is because I feel very much trapped and heavy."

Cindy recalled her past experiences when she had debated hotly with Kent on the topics they disagreed upon. Then she was saddened as she talked.

"It is painful to talk about disagreements," I interjected. "Arguments invoke the rational mind. For Kent to keep agreeing with you over the 'rightness' or 'wrongness' of his arguments and be reminded of the hurt he had been experiencing in giving way to you, would be a continual blow to his already bruised ego."

"Once again, you have succeeded in opening my mind," Cindy remarked. "You seem to know how Kent thinks. I have been cracking my head as to how I should talk to Kent over what went wrong. I believe this is why our communication has always been a roadblock. I did attempt to pull Kent out of his negative patterns in the early beginning. He found out and remarked that there is no way I could know what he had been going through."

I encouraged Cindy to talk freely. Facilitating her to recast her problem as an affliction and to focus on the effects of the problem was helpful in healing.

"According to Kent's relatives he was very cheerful and talkative in his younger days," Cindy said. "No one knows why he has become so quiet and negative now. However, I notice that he talks well during marketing and sales. It is only to his parents that he hardly talks. Something must have happened during his growing-up years. His mother looks scary to me when she blows up. I am sure his mother could have caned him very badly in his younger days. Kent said that when he was small he couldn't fight back. At one stage his mother told me that she regretted the caning and told me that she had to discipline him only because he misbehaved. His mother has improved since ... but now Kent uses the cane on his own son!" Cindy sighed.

Rapid healing seemed to have set in after the second session. The next morning, while Kent was preparing to go to work, Cindy experienced a sudden and unexplained urge to do something for him. This was something that she had never done in the past, nor ever thought of doing. She asked Kent which shirt he wanted to wear, took his choice out of the wardrobe and buttoned it up for him. While doing so, she was experiencing a flashback of a childhood scene of her mum buttoning the shirt for her dad.

I was amazed at her healing process! To my mind there are several little things a woman can do to melt a man's heart. Buttoning his shirt for him was indeed one of them!

"This is what my mother has done for my dad. I realize that it is the same emotional support that Kent needed. It is so simple. Kent clearly asked for it and I did not get it earlier. He once told me that I do not know how to become a woman ... and I got angry with him!" Cindy recalled soberly.

Kent was initially dumbfounded at her buttoning act. To Cindy's dismay, he slighted her behavior as being strange. He asked if anything was wrong with her. She remained silent and tears rolled down her cheeks while she completed her task.

Next, Kent was leaving for work and, at the door, Cindy asked him suddenly: "Can you give me a hug?" Kent was stunned for a second time that morning. Nonetheless, he gave her a good hug. She closed her eyes and it seemed as if her body melted into his, like a dream. As she sent him off in his car, her tears continued to flow.

"I am now beginning to see his sincerity. His suffering throughout these four weeks has indicated that he does care. He does try to soul-search but encounters emptiness and frustration. He is equally lost, and is struggling to find his own path too."

Five days later, Cindy had a breakthrough experience. A message suddenly flashed through her mind and she recalled a passage from a book by Dr. Brian Weiss:

"All is love ... all is love ... with love comes understanding, with understanding comes patience. And then time stops. And everything is now!"

Cindy suddenly understood that Kent had actually loved her throughout their marriage but she was so blinded that she couldn't receive his love.

"His frustration stemmed from the fact that no matter what he did or said, he wasn't understood by me ... and I truly didn't. I couldn't even understand his simple feeling of emptiness. My blindness has been coated with my disappointments. He is unable to express the love language that I have been yearning for. I used to be in the sea of hatred and too swamped with the feeling of injustice and too many disappointments. I was lost, and have always questioned whether there is love in our relationship to begin with. I had too many doubts about our relationship. I do expect a lot from Kent, most of which he can't deliver, and I keep forcing my expectations onto him. Ah well ... he did ask for my unconditional support on a few previous occasions and I didn't get what he meant."

The healing process continued at a rapid pace. I observed that Cindy was noticing not only what was going on around her, but also what was going on within her.

"Slowly, I have come to understand Kent's behavior. You are right that I have to work towards the healing of his perception that he is not cared for and unloved. Subconsciously he does know I care, but he is also aware that I don't understand him. Hence, he decides to break away from this marriage."

On the following morning, at 5:15 am, Cindy suddenly woke up and wrote: "I have finally understood what Kent needs. It is my encouragement, care and support. It's just the emotional support that a spouse would usually provide to her warrior husband who needs to go out to the field to fight in the war. Gosh! How come I didn't realize all this while? Mum always did that for my dad!"

After sending her husband off to work that morning, she gathered her courage to send Kent a telephone message: "I have finally come to the realization that I have understood why things are turning out this way. From now on I will give you my support, my care and my love."

Session 3: Marital Hurt

On the same afternoon (16 October), Cindy came to my clinic for another therapy session. By now her emotions had stabilized. She appeared cheerful and had become increasingly fascinated with the process of thinking in pictures. Stepping into the experience of blending guided imagery with innovative thought had opened her to a new realm of healing possibilities.

In this session, Cindy had chosen to address her issue of sexual intimacy with her husband. She had earlier perceived this to be the major contributor to her marriage failure and did not want to rest till she got to the root of the problem. She believed that doing so would put her in a better position to help Kent thereafter.

"It cannot be a situation that is on-going. Just because we always quarrel doesn't mean that the mind cannot concentrate on intimacy and Kent couldn't give me an answer on that."

Cindy said it with bitterness and hurt.

"Maybe he doesn't know the answer himself," she continued. "He always refers back to the time before our marriage when we

36

have already been quarrelling, and says that our quarrels have distracted him from his sexual interest. However, I come from the angle that this cannot account for the gravity of the problem."

I silently disagreed.

To me, Kent's erectile dysfunction was obviously a product of their constant emotional conflicts. When waters churned up during quarrels and arguments became still subsequently, the calmness was probably confined to the surface. Kent had probably submerged his bruised feelings in the interest of harmony, and these feelings lingered to fester in the fertile substrate of his unconscious mind. He was already overwhelmed with his career stress. He was probably preoccupied with personal strife to prove himself, and had no room for developing an interest in sexual intimacy. In all likelihood, his gnawing anger, insecurity and resentment had been building up to a crescendo to cripple his erectile function even before marriage.

As Cindy relaxed into a hypnotic state, she regressed back to the night when her marriage was consummated. She had set the intention of reliving the time when she had to face the ordeal of Kent's erectile dysfunction. Intention is a form of directed will, and by telling herself that she was going to accomplish a particular objective, she was out to make this therapy session a success.

"I am back to the night when the intimacy first took place." Suddenly I saw Cindy's facial muscles tensing up.

"It is painful ..."

"Tell me more."

"It's very painful." Her eyebrows were contracting. The eyelids tightened and the upper lip was elevated while her body stiffened. She subsequently recalled, after the session, how the degree of tightness of her genitalia on that eventful night worked

37

against the intimate process. Even on subsequent occasions, it took her a significant duration to relax adequately for penetration.

"What is going on?"

"It is very uncomfortable. I am pushing him away. He tries and tries ... and gives the final push. It goes in, but then ... it is very painful." She frowned.

"Focus on the pain, tell me the feelings that are coming up."

There was a long pause.

"I don't like it. Emm ... it's so painful ... I feel frustrated ... and a bit lost. Why is it like that?" She sounded perplexed.

"Tell me your thoughts now."

There was another pause.

"I am scared. I don't know what I am scared of, but I am very sad. (pause) This is not love at all! This is pain ... it's awful!"

"Are you not happy that he is finally able to do it?"

"No ... Not happy at all. It is not supposed to be like that. I expect gentleness." Cindy responded while remaining fully focused on the trauma of the event.

"This is so harsh and rough. He is not considerate at all. It is very painful. I told him about it but he is rushing into it when I am not ready."

It suddenly alerted me to the fact that a window of opportunity had just opened up for healing. My training had taught me that at any given moment in the regression process, the patient had the power to say that this is not how my story is going to end. This is the core of the "reframing" process. Such an approach would provide room for the patient to reframe her story and create room for healing.

Reframing a regression script would be analogous to playing the role of a choreographer in the therapy process. The challenge was to guide the patient to compose an imagined sequence of actions and events for her to re-enact so that the imagined or newly created event would fulfill her psychological need. Immediately I started to help her to restructure her inner self with the necessary imagery.

"I want you to visualize Kent being in front of you."

"Yes, I see him there." Cindy responded promptly.

"Tell him you are not ready and not to rush into it."

"I am not ready, ... I don't feel I like it ... Can you just wait? (pause) He indicated that he could not wait any longer. He is being very forceful."

There was an upset expression on Cindy's face. I then guided her to plead with Kent for gentleness.

"Can you please do it slowly? Relax and don't rush into it," Cindy whispered softly to Kent.

It soon became apparent that one of the most powerful functions of hypnodrama was the capacity for Cindy to enact not only what had happened on that emotionally traumatic night, but also what never happened. What never happened was the "psychological truth" for Cindy and that carried much more importance than the "historical truth" for the purpose of healing.

"How is Kent responding now?"

"He takes a deep breath and calms down a little bit."

"Help him to calm down further so that you both can enjoy the intimacy."

"Relax, Kent ... take more care ... Just relax slowly," Cindy pleaded. "Yes ... I am enjoying it more now ... so is Kent. He is able to respond now."

The use of the reframing approach turned out to be a beautiful act of transformation and created an ecstatic experience under trance. It was an important moment in inner healing. Cindy could express her passionate feelings to her husband in a way that she hadn't in the past nine years. She succeeded in getting Kent to respond sensually in a manner that ultimately fulfilled her dreams.

"He feels very loved ... I do not feel the pain now," Cindy continued, looking relaxed and happy. I then guided her to communicate her feelings of sensuality to Kent, and reach a climax. "It was pleasurable ... I want more ... I feel free ... I am surrendering ... released ... and satisfied."

Eventually I brought Cindy out of trance. How hypnodrama can extend the scope of healing in regression therapy is analogous to what electric power tools have done for carpentry. The essence of integration in Cindy's case was made possible by the enacting of a "corrective scene" so that she could re-live the traumatic situation by re-experiencing what had happened in a more positive fashion. Bringing unspoken and unfulfilled fantasies into her explicit awareness was all that was needed. The theoretical basis of the approach was to create a space, where she could live out alternative realities on her mental stage, and try out a different way of behaving within a safe environment. Rather than purely recollecting what actually happened on that night, she obtained clarity on what she had always hoped for, even though it was not real. The re-enacted scene represented the psychological world of Cindy in which her imaginative expression allowed the completion of an unresolved conflict through re-experiencing it with a corrective reframe. With that, healing took place.

There was a short moment of embarrassment as Cindy emerged from the trance state. Yet more importantly, she appreciated the connection of her heart to a source of wisdom greater than her mind. Her hopes had rekindled. She could visualize her husband's conformity to her needs and the possibility of a mutual enjoyment of the intimate experience. By replaying an unfortunate event, Cindy now experienced a more empowered and satisfactory ending.

Following the session, a series of thoughts emerged.

"Does it mean that things can turn out to be a more positive way?" she asked. "I begin to feel that it can happen, and I feel very strongly that Kent does love me. He really does. I guess too many aspects of his life are meddling with his mind and he cannot surface his emotions."

CHAPTER TWO

Marriage Crisis II: Moving Forward

Dr. Peter Mack

"What most of us need, almost more than anything, is the courage and humility really to ask for help, from the depths of our hearts ... to ask for purification and healing, to ask for the power to understand the meaning of our suffering and transform it; at a relative level to ask for the growth in our lives of clarity, of peace, of discernment..."

Sogyal Rinpoche
In: Tibetan Book of Living and Dying, 2002

The gloom that had previously plagued Cindy had vanished. At the next therapy session, on the afternoon of 17 October 2012, she appeared cheerful. She came in a dark-brownish T-shirt with a shiny red flowery pattern, looking bright and calm.

Session 4: Unconditional Love

As Cindy relaxed into a trance state on the couch, she experienced a feeling of peace within. The theme of freedom that surfaced at her very first therapy session came up again in her emerging thoughts.

"I have done everything I can consciously, but it is not good enough," she began. "I can't get the result that I want. It is just one more step to go, but it is so difficult."

There was a pause.

"I am reaching out with my hand to Kent," Cindy said emotionally, and was beginning to cry. "He is trying to reach out with his hand to me too ... but he cannot grasp it tightly enough."

Catharsis set in. I waited for one and a half minutes. She drifted spontaneously to two other scenes that were repetitive, one after another.

Firstly, Cindy saw herself alone, seated in a dark room with no windows, with a light shining on her from the ceiling. She was staring at the wall in deep thought. On the table she saw a notebook. "I am writing down something ... as if I am studying. Whenever my thoughts come I write them down. It is a Mathematics question ... with some calculations. I don't know why they are bothering me. I am just studying ..."

Then the imagery suddenly drifted to another scene.

"I am at the seaside again. Very nice ... the wind blows. I am enjoying my walk, my stroll. It's very quiet. I like the sound of the waves. I am by myself ... very peaceful.

The sequence of the two seemingly unrelated scenes immediately struck me as symbolic of her inner self. The dark room was where Cindy was struggling to search for answers whereas the beach was where intuitive solutions to her problems would freely flow. I took the opportunity to help her develop this positive part of her inner self.

"Describe the beach to me."

"A sandy beach ... and it is between six and seven o'clock in the evening. It's sunset time. It is a bit hazy and I feel happy and light."

"Listen to the sound of the waves and describe your feelings."

"Nice and contented. I am free now and very relaxed. I am myself and have a lot of room in my heart ... I feel very peaceful."

Cindy later elaborated on her yearning for freedom. She had for a long time been struggling with her inner urge to please other people, particularly her mother. She believed that the lesson to learn was to understand people. With her improved understanding of Kent after a fortnight of therapy, she noticed a shift in her own consciousness. She was now better able to let go and stop intervening in the way in which Kent disciplined their children, even though she felt he was somewhat harsh.

"So you have found the answer to your freedom? What is the lesson you have learned?"

"It's about love ... I love everyone in this world. I want everybody to love me and be good. I want myself and everybody to be in peace ... and harmony."

"How do you intend to achieve that?

"I just wish my husband Kent and my children to be around, be happy and have what they like and enjoy. I am happy to see them smile and will be more contented in this manner."

"How far are you able to achieve that?"

"Not far. It's just right in front ... just there."

"Do you know what to do for Kent now?"

"Actually ... yes. I have not been able to let him go, but he is really happier without me. I still want to hold on to him."

Cindy went into catharsis again.

"It's very difficult to let him go. I still want to keep him and he feels trapped."

I felt amazed at Cindy's insight and the sudden change in her temperament at the perceptual level. It had been a consistent observation in my experience that the patient's mind, if given the unrestricted space under trance, has an incredible power to move towards an enlightened state, beyond her present state of growth.

"What can you do to make him feel less trapped and happier if he stays with you?" I asked.

There was a pause.

"I don't know …" She sounded stuck. I waited for a moment and decided to guide her to develop greater awareness through her inner wisdom.

"Ask your Inner Advisor to help you with an answer."

Cindy quickly responded upon that prompt. "He says just let him be. Let him be himself." Following a pause, she continued: "Actually he doesn't want to leave me. He is still there. Kent is still there …"

Cindy was ecstatic as she visualized the happiness in Kent and his reluctance to leave.

"Ask him what you should do to make him happy and yet be himself."

"He says let him do whatever he wants to do. He says he loves me still, and he says it's alright … he is not going away from me after all!"

For a moment, this revelation seemed too good to be true! Nonetheless, I embraced this response as it was bringing on significant healing on Cindy's part.

"Are you prepared to accept his proposal?"

"Yes. He smiles … and I tell him, I believe you can make it. I trust you and will give you my support. I can take care of the kids … no problem, I can do it."

I allowed the hypnodrama to continue.

"He is more confident now, and I am giving him a hug. He is hugging me back and is crying. He says he loves me too, and he says he is sorry. (catharsis) I tell him it is okay as we all make mistakes."

Cindy was crying very loudly at this stage. I waited to give her time to dive in all the way to experience her emotions fully. I felt this was important for her to obtain her needed healing.

A few minutes later, her crying stopped and I asked: "What happens next?"

"We both calm down. I hold his hand. He says nothing and holds my hand in return. I wish him all the best and reassure him that he is free to go and I will give him full support from now onwards. He receives my message."

It was a moving moment. Cindy was beginning to let go of Kent psychologically and she sensed his happiness. As I was concluding the session, I brought her back to the same imagery of the beach that she always loved, and configured a healing script.

"As you stand on the shore, the water stretches as far as you can see on the horizon. It is twilight and you can't tell the ocean from the sky. Waves are flowing towards you, breaking into foam, creeping up to your feet and sliding back. Listen to the waves. As each wave pounds on the rocks, you stand spellbound by the shore as you are also able to discern the rhythmic crash of water on water, and water on sand. Every wave that comes brings with it healing power. Listen to the cry of the seagulls as they circle in the sky. Feel the breeze blowing at your face as they bring delight, hope and joy. Continue to stay relaxed on the beach. This is the place where you find enlightenment and the answer to your relationship with Kent. This is the same place when you are able to reconcile with Kent in soul and spirit."

After the session, Cindy felt perplexed with her repeated visualization of the seaside scene. Several days later, she suddenly woke up one morning and messaged me to describe how she saw the seaside symbolism falling into place.

"Water, waves, sea, beach, swimming, cool weather, breeze, sunset and sunrise, cooking dinner at twilight, the peace of watching television alone ..." she recounted. "The mix of all these scenes and images is symbolic of my affinity with water, which has a calming effect on me."

Cindy's insight was particularly interesting because my personal understanding of the symbolism of water had a different slant. To me, water represents all potentialities of existence that precede every form and creation. Contact with water goes with dissolution into a more undifferentiated state. This is followed by a new birth. Immersion in water fertilizes and multiplies the potentialities of life. This was why I believed that Cindy's repeated visualization of water scenes signified an on-going regenerative process for her. While water dissolved the form of things, it also purified and enhanced renewal for her. Deep within, the imagery of the roaring sea and the waves crashing on the rocks had helped her to rediscover her connection with the universe.

Evidence of healing continued to manifest after the session.

"I have come to certainty that my life lesson is learning to give and receive unconditionally, that is, unconditional love," she said. "It's painful really ... to love unconditionally without asking for anything in return. My understanding of unconditional love is that it means to let go of the person freely without controlling. It means freedom, no strings and no attachment. It means wishing the person happiness and peace, whatever the circumstances. The word 'love' is sounding so strong now ... I have never realized that I am able to love this man so strongly.

"Love, as in the form of letting go, is the hardest. I keep holding on to Kent till he feels trapped and unable to do the things that he wants to do in his own way. He has told me before what he needs – unconditional support without questioning. He has since come to the conclusion that I will not be able to do that because I always keep asking him, Why? Is it justifiable? Does it make sense?

"I think Kent's life lesson is to learn to open up and realize truthfully that he is always being loved; that his life is not like what he thinks. He is to accept his life contentedly and learn to be appreciative of his surroundings. Our lives are intertwined and planned to fit each other's needs, and I have to be the one that acts to make him realize that.

"Since young, I have been very well taken care of and have been shown the way to care and love. Now it's the time for me to give back what I have received and put in practice what I have been taught. The repetitive flashbacks of scenes of interaction between my mum and dad, my sister and brother-in-law, as well as those between my other siblings, are giving me the signs and directions.

"It's clear to me now! One way to go through this path is to allow space for each other. It's the freedom to be ourselves. It is not about changing ourselves to meet each other's expectations. It is to learn what we are supposed to learn, and we both will be there for the kids always. I will live my life meaningfully from now onwards and leave the universe to unfold my life plan."

Those were inspiring words. It seemed that the discovery of meaning had turned on the clockwork of healing. She had understood that the meaning of her existence needed to resonate with her physical, social, psychological and spiritual realms in order to create a rich fabric of life. Each part of her inner psyche had been establishing a continuous dialogue with the other parts to provide an avenue through which she could get in touch with her greater whole. The stormy sea and peaceful waters, the sunrise and the twilight, the beach and the sound of the waves were all part of her greater web of being.

Another five days passed.

Cindy's feeling of emotional bond to the marriage relationship began to diminish. "Strangely, I look for the sense of attachment within me and it seems to have drifted quite far away. I do not feel so tight anymore and there is room for other things. I think I am moving in the right direction and meditation has helped a lot in calming my mind."

Cindy had understood that letting go meant leaving things as they were. It was not about annihilating them or throwing them away. It was through her practice of meditation that she began to understand the origin of her suffering – her attachment to desire.

Letting go of Kent involved a reluctant and gradual withdrawal of energy, love and attachment of him on Cindy's part. When she faced and accepted the reality internally, her external behavior started to change. I cautioned her that there might be waves of sadness shaking her up as she came to terms with the change. She would need to figure out what aspects of her life she needed to relinquish in order to move forward to become the woman she wanted to become.

Another positive development took place in the meanwhile. Cindy took her first swimming exercise one morning at 7:00 am. She sensed a great sense of achievement on her part. The low temperature of the water did not deter her. She began to appreciate her mind power as her body temperature rapidly equilibrated with that of the cold pool water. "It's all in the mind," she remarked.

"Many little things that I have done so far indicate a change in my behavior. As I now wake up my son in the morning for school and send him out the door, I see that he is very happy with my action. By just observing him drink his milk at breakfast and helping him to put on his socks and shoes, I realize that these little tasks can ease the little boy's emotion and irritation of having to rush to school. I can sense the feeling of peace really ...

with all these changes. I sincerely hope all these positive behaviors of mine will stay and grow into a permanent transformation."

Session 5: Life's Turning Point

On 31 October, Cindy came to my clinic in a pink shirt and black pants, looking a little bit tired. For the past week, she had been struggling hard to figure out her life purpose, and had come to the conclusion that she had been fighting against her destiny all the while.

"It was precisely because I have not believed in my destiny that I have been doing all these things for the past nine years," she said. "I have come one big circle back to the same problems with this relationship issue. Right from day one, the relationship problem has been there. So it is either something that has failed to break away or I am still trying to understand better in order to move on." This statement gave me a sense of increasing self-awareness on Cindy's part.

After a short breathing exercise on the therapy couch, Cindy went rapidly into a hypnotic state, and she said: "I experience happiness, peace and freedom ..."

"Tell me your thoughts that are associated with these emotions," I prompted.

"I do not have to be struggling like I am now. I can just take it one step at a time and go with the flow. It's like feeling the breeze while enjoying the journey. At times, when I pass through a meadow, I just enjoy looking at the flowers, the leaves, and the colorful scenery. At other times, when it is raining and with a little storm, I will just look at the rain outside the window. I tell myself that soon the rain will be over and the sun will come up again and we can go out and play."

Following these thoughts, she regressed back to a scene in her younger years. It was a remarkable experience, one that allowed me to understand the many subtle, covert ways in which she felt wounded, while she was growing up.

"I am seventeen years old. My father has just passed away in China." She began to sob. I listened with interest.

"I do not know what my feelings are. I am taking my afternoon nap and my brother wakes me up with the shocking news that Dad has passed away. I don't know how to cry and am asking myself what does that mean. After that, my mum tells me I have to be independent henceforth. I register clearly in my mind the word 'independence'. I am the youngest child in the family. My siblings are all grown up and I am still in secondary school. They decide to send me to Sydney to study. It's tough. It is the first time I am away from home."

Cindy began crying. I waited. Intuitively, I anticipated that a disturbing story was about to emerge.

"I feel very lonely. I am being placed in a school in which there are only three Asian students. It is a culture shock ... I do not know how to speak or express myself in English then. When I listen to the radio, I cannot understand anything at all. I feel like an alien. The word 'independence' comes to my mind again. For the first time in my life I look at the newspapers, get a job and go to work. I am working in a McDonald's restaurant. I earn my own money. I feel very happy and proud of myself."

"What happens next?"

"I am staying with my third brother in the same house. He also feels very lonely. He goes to work while I go to school. I come home and cook dinner and he washes the plates. I wash the clothes and he irons them. Two years pass. I cannot get myself to mix around with Caucasian students. I have only a handful of Asian friends."

There was a tone of sadness in Cindy's voice.

"In the university I meet a group of friends. I feel the closeness, the support and the caring. That shapes me up. One of them brings me to the Buddhist Society. We are in the Society's committee meeting ... life starts moving. I learn a lot from them.

"I enjoy the four years of university life throughout. It is the best time of my life. What happens next is that I am not doing well in my studies. I am doing Industrial Chemistry, but halfway through, I dislike the course. So I cut it short, skip the Honors year and complete the degree earlier.

"I go home and manage to find a job related to Industrial Chemistry in the marketing department of a company that deals with laboratory equipment testing. I do not like it and I quit. Then my brother gets me into a banking job through his contacts. I am in the SMA Bank as a trainee. I am in one of the bank's best performing branches. I am the only lady out of seven or eight guys. I am very gung-ho, being the only overseas graduate. People look up at me. I go and meet clients, understand how the business works, write reports, grant credits and I learn a lot.

"Then I meet Henry ... He likes me. I don't know how the feeling develops. He helps me out in many things. Our relationship gets very intense. Mum finds out about it and says 'no' to it because he is six years older than I, and also because he is a Hepatitis B carrier. My father was also a Hepatitis B carrier and died from liver cancer. So Mum considers him unacceptable.

"At the same time other things happen in the family. My third brother just had an affair that is leading to a divorce. The family is upset and Mum puts a stop to my relationship with Henry. So I told her I want to go back to school and study."

The last statement struck a chord. The symbolism of "school" and "life" are on opposite sides of a polarity. School is about learning lessons and life is about undergoing testing. Cindy had just faced a test in life that taught her a lesson! It struck me that her going back to school would indicate that she now wanted to learn her lesson again before taking the next test in her life.

"Mum objects to my decision," Cindy continued. "She says a woman doesn't need such a high educational level. Yet, the stronger her objection the more I want to go back to school. (sobbing) I want to be independent and I am breaking the norm. Mum says she is not going to support me if I do so. I tell her that it's fine and I can survive on my own. I book the air ticket and I get myself a loan for my course in Finance. I don't care ... I just want to show other people I can do it. With my own savings I am going ahead. She is broken-hearted and she can't stop me.

"I am very lonely. I take a cab from the airport and somehow I find my own accommodation. I work and study at the same time. I am lucky to get a job as a customer service officer at a bank. So, I work in the day and attend lectures at night. Mum misses me very much. She later comes to Sydney to visit me. I used to hate her negative attitude towards educational needs for women. My family members say I am very stubborn. I know and I understand that there is only so much a woman can do in society, but my character cannot be changed.

"Life in Sydney is good. I am there for only one year and I get back my life. Before returning home to Jakarta, I have a job waiting for me as a corporate banker in an Indonesian bank. So I have it all planned out. However, only seven to eight months into the job, the whole chaos happened ... the Indonesian Riots. The thought of loneliness creeps up again.

"This time round, my third brother and I somehow are together again. We are fearful of the sight of the shop houses being robbed and burned. All the rioters are very scary." Cindy was crying badly.

At that point I began to recall with shudders what I read in the newspapers about the Indonesian Riots in May 1998. It happened at the height of the Asian Financial Crisis that started in 1997. Mass violence occurred throughout Indonesia and was particularly rife in Medan, Jakarta and Surakata. The regional crisis precipitated major economic problems in the country including mass unemployment and food shortages. More than a thousand people were reported dead in the riots and several hundred Indonesian-Chinese women were raped. Tens of thousands of ethnic Chinese fled the country after the event.

"Anytime the group can just budge in and I will be gone ..." Cindy cried out in fear. "I hear people shouting and screaming while the houses are burning. My brother is very scared. He is very worried for me. We are the only two left inside the house. (sobbing) My other siblings are stuck at the airport. They have driven their wives, kids, mums and mother-in-laws there to take a flight to Singapore but are stuck."

"How is this so?"

"The Indonesian-Chinese have become the target of violence by the local gangsters. Chinese-owned business stores are looted. It is too chaotic ... too scary! The phone keeps ringing. The place we have been staying is at a strategic location because we are en route to the airport. Friends and relatives call in to monitor the situation. My second brother flies off eventually with my eldest brother. My eldest brother manages to get air tickets for all of us ... but how are we to get to the airport? We have to find our own way! It is dark ... about 5:00 am and a decision has to be made. My third brother says firmly to me that we have to go to the airport now.

"There is this worker who is with us. So my third brother asks him: Do you know how to drive? He says yes. I don't even know how we get our passports. We get up to a lorry at around 6:00 am.

It is dark. He says he knows how to drive, but he drives at thirty to forty kilometers per hour. It is a very long journey to the airport. On the way are troops of rioters and people and I don't dare to look at them. There is burning and I can see smoke here and there.

"Somehow we reach the airport safely. I have only a few pieces of clothing with me. We fly safely to Singapore. I feel very lucky to get away ... I read all the news about the riots in the newspapers ... friends and people are talking about the incidents and rape cases. People are holding grudges. Maybe I can forgive because I have got away ..."

Cindy had just narrated a very painful recollection of a nightmarish experience and I allowed her to do it freely. I decided to end the session at this point. The story-telling would have created new meanings from her past and her story would influence the way she viewed herself and the world around her. At this stage of the therapy, I felt it was as important to learn about her meaning systems as much as about her behavior.

I realized that Cindy's new meaning system had helped her to understand her life experiences from two perspectives. Firstly, Cindy realized that her third brother had consistently played a significant role in her life, being present by her side during her most critical times and the turning points in her life. He had taught her how to analyze and solve mathematical problems during school years. He was with her during the escape from the Indonesian Riots. Furthermore, his own relationship and marital issues had left an imprint on her mind. For a moment, Cindy was surprised that till now she had never seen her brother's presence in her life from that perspective.

Secondly, loneliness was the theme behind Cindy's regression story and a denominator of many other aspects of her life. It was the driver for her personal achievements, as she wanted to show others she could succeed alone and with little help. Loneliness had shaped her early adult identity with a sense of independence and the urge to prove herself. Over time she had learned to become an overly assertive character. Yet, I believe her past had prepared her well for who she was to become.

Session 6: Metaphor for Life

I noticed that by now Cindy's complexion had brightened up. A week later, on 6 November, I saw her again. This time, she appeared more relaxed and with a soothing gaze that looked directly at me without staring or blinking. With a gleam in her eyes and a regular breathing rhythm, she reassured me confidently that she was well on her path of recovery, and close to embarking on another new chapter in her life journey.

Cindy had just passed her seventh weekend since the beginning of her marriage crisis without an emotional breakdown. She was clear on what she needed for her sixth therapy session – guidance on detecting her life purpose.

After a short induction, she regressed back to her favorite seaside imagery again. I could sense that she was very relaxed.

"It is towards evening and I am just enjoying myself taking a stroll alone at the beach. I am feeling very peaceful and happy," she said in a slow soft tone. "It is a sandy beach. I just like to sit at the beach and feel the breeze and listen to the sound of the waves. I feel very serene and very peaceful. It is sunset time, probably around 6:00 pm."

"Describe the sun to me."

"It is round and half-set behind the sea. The color is a bit orange. I am very happy."

"What thoughts are associated with the happiness?"

"Freedom ... there is a lot of room in the heart."

The serene manner in which Cindy introduced the theme of freedom this time immediately highlighted a contrast with the tumultuous state of her mind during her first therapy session.

"Listen to the sound of the waves and reflect over the beach scene to see if it has a meaning related to your life purpose."

"Life is beautiful," she began. "Life is full of ups and downs. That is why there is impermanence. Life is about letting go and following through with that. It is about following the ups and then following the downs. It can be a joy to give and give sincerely."

"What special meaning does the seaside have with regards to your purpose of life?"

There was a long pause. Suddenly Cindy spoke up as if in an epiphany.

"The sea gives me the calm. I feel peaceful. It is endless and boundless. Look at the waves … it is like the eternal life. I can travel as far as I want to. I can achieve as much as I want to. There is no limit. I must do what I want to do and not be lazy. I have to go out of my comfort zone. I can do anything I want and there is a possibility to everything as long as I put in the effort. I never know."

It was a beautifully enacted verse. I decided to lead her on.

"Which areas of life would you put in your effort next?"
"Everything … my career, relationships, kids, parents, siblings and of course, my husband. There is no limit to the list. I do not know the outcome until I reach there. Things keep changing. You put in the effort … one moment it's up, and next moment it's down. It is impermanent; there is no fixed situation. That is why it is not fate. When you travel with it you go on top of the wave and ride on it. That's the beauty. It's an adventure and there is no worry. I never know what to expect. That is why love is beautiful. It should not be dull … it should be colorful. Whatever challenges come I will just handle it there and then.

"The next issue that comes up is another new way of looking at things. It is a wonderful feeling if one can float on top of the waves, just like a surfer taking the opportunity of the waves. At times you fall back, but you go up later and swing back again. Just like the surfer who learns by mistake. Yes, the sense of achievement is to be able to surf on top of the waves. It is the act of balancing. At times, the waves hit the cliffs, but it has to move back again. There are times the waters are calm. That's why I like to watch the waves. They are never the same. As I learn to listen to the sound of the waves, it tells me a lot of things."

"Such as?"

"Going with the flow ... learning the tactics. There are times when I need to mellow down ... I will mellow down. There are times when I need to fight ... I must fight. There are times when I can even dance with it. There is a song with the sound of the waves. As I listen with my heart, there is a tune to it."

"How does this realization impact on you and your future?"

"It is about choice. Every moment is a choice. It is a choice to break out of my comfort zone and out of my cave to feel the external world. It is actually very beautiful. I don't have to be so afraid ... I need to fully connect with my children. I have neglected them in many ways."

This therapy session ended with a wonderful feeling on Cindy's part. Her intuitive perception that surfaced while under trance had been amazing. Although most of what she said was metaphoric, it set her towards a path of deep reflection.

By now, there were positive signs of transformational changes. After the session Cindy suddenly went back to the dance studio to practice her ballet again. She loved ballet as a child but she had stopped practicing it for the past twenty-two years. After the class, she felt refreshed and fully charged. In the meanwhile she continued with her daily meditation and her morning swim twice weekly. Her appearance had brightened up and her friends had recently noticed a rapid improvement in her emotional state.

Session 7: Past Life in China

Cindy returned the next day, 7 November, requesting for a special session on past life healing. Hypnotic induction had become very straightforward by now, but she felt that she needed to understand her past life connection.

Under trance, a feeling of fear emerged. I asked her to focus on the fear, amplified it and used it as an affect bridge. She instantly connected with a past life of herself in ancient China.

"I see myself lying down in bed on a white pillow, feeling very helpless and weak. Yeah ... I am back in ancient China during one of the older dynasties. I am in my late thirties or early forties. My hair is bundled up. There is a metal basin with a towel next to my bed. My dress is white with lace. I have a young servant and she is standing next to me. I think I am in pain."

"Tell me about your pain."

"I am not sure why I am feeling the pain, but I am sweating and my maid is helping me to put the wet towel on my forehead."

"Describe your maid to me."

"She is young, in her twenties. Unlike me, her hair is not bundled up. There is a black ribbon tied to her hair and she has a long hairpin with some ornaments on it. She wears black-colored shoes with a slightly curved tip. Her outfit consists of a tunic and pants with an outer skirt covering all the way to the ankles. I can't see her face."

"What are you suffering from?"

"I see myself lying down with my head on an old dynasty wooden pillow. I don't know what I am suffering, but ... I can get out of the bed."

"Feel the pain and describe its location on your body."

"The pain is on the middle of my chest. I am walking now ... I am sitting next to a round table. I feel better now and am no longer in pain. I am drinking my tea. I look very elegant and very pretty in my dress."

"What happens next?"

"I walk towards the window and the door. It seems like I am waiting for somebody. Only the maid and I are in the room. I am combing my hair, freshening up myself. The mirror is oval-shaped and has a decorative wooden frame with some curly patterns. There are some side drawers. I look very pretty ... I am instructing my maid on how to comb my hair."

"What are your emotions at this stage?

"Quite peaceful and serene."

"What thoughts are on your mind?"

"I am very happy ... waiting for my husband to come back and I want to get ready to welcome him home. I am looking forward to meeting him."

"What happens next?"

There was a pause. It seemed that her warrior husband had just returned, wearing his armor.

"Hmm ... oh yeah, he is in an army suit ... the armor outfit with all the war weapons. He looks tired. He takes off his suit."

I listened to the past life story with intrigue. Cindy's story fitted well with the insight she had acquired during an "Ah-Ha" moment three weeks ago – that what Kent really needed from her in the past nine years was the emotional support that a spouse would normally "provide to her warrior husband who needs to go out to the field to fight in the war."

"I cannot see his face. He takes off his helmet. His hair is bundled up with a pony-tail in a manly style. He is drinking his tea. ... We are having our meal on the table."

There was a pause and Cindy's voice turned very shy. "He insists on making love … and I entertained," she said softly.

I was alerted again. The lack of intimacy had been the sore point in her current marriage, whereas the opposite seemed to prevail in her past life!

"What are your emotions now?"

"Filled with love … I can sense he is very tired. He needs to release. It is okay … it is just a man's thing. He is very appreciative of my support. It's over now. He puts back his clothes. It is a white robe. I am washing his feet. I just do whatever a wife is supposed to do. I listen to him and comfort him."

"What happens next?

"He says it is a tough battle that he just fought. He has been away for twenty days. Now he is making the trip out again to fight another war. He is getting his gear."

"How do you feel when you hear the news?"

"I feel okay and do not feel sad. I give him the confidence. I understand he is doing this for the country and wish him all the best. I will wait for him to come back and rest assured that everything will be fine. There is no burden … it is mutual understanding. I feel happy, contented and very complete."

"Has he left now?"

"I see him walking out. He rides on the horse and leaves."

"As you watch him leaving do you have any emotions?"

"No, I have total confidence in him."

Cindy's feeling of experiencing a past life brought on a lot of excitement for her. For the first time she began to appreciate the freeing of her mind from the five hindrances in Buddhism – craving, aversion, sloth, agitation and doubt. She started to experience a very peaceful state and her senses became very sharp.

A week later, she developed new insights into the meaning of her past life in China. She had always felt very lonely because her husband in that past life was a warrior who left her alone at home while he fought in battles. She was a most loving and submissive spouse. Hence in the current life she had wanted to experience a role reversal.

Session 8: Bliss and Harmony

Another week passed. Cindy had gathered momentum in her recovery and she wanted to continue to explore her past life at greater depth. It was on the afternoon of 20 November and she appeared in high spirits.

After a short induction, she quickly regressed back to another scene in ancient China.

"I am in my mid-twenties and see myself in white clothes. I am sitting somewhere inside a house and doing knitting. It is a nice house with a sharp segregation between the bedroom and the living room. My embroidery work is flowery in pattern. It's red and glittering. My hair is done up as a bun. There is a lacy ribbon, some ornaments and a hairpin on my hair ... very elegant. There are writings and calligraphy in big characters on a paper picture hung on the wall. The tables and stools are mostly made of bamboo while some others are wooden."

"What are you doing now?"

"I am looking out of the window and waiting for someone .... Oh, my husband is returning from a long journey. He is wearing his armor and carrying his shield and sword. He takes out his things from his bag. I am happy that he is back. He is very big-sized and masculine.

"He says he is very tired, but he looks very strong. So I massaged his back and percussed his shoulder for him."

"What thoughts are coming through your mind?"

63

There was a pause.

"My husband is happy to see me. He gets comforted. We are eating and drinking from brass cups and teapots. I find that I tend not to ask what he does outside. I am very obliging and just serve him. I am folding his clothes, cleaning his stuff. I see a bronze mirror with a curved surface. There is another small mirror that I look at myself with and use for makeup. It is resting on a dressing table. I feel emotionally alright and have no worries. I just live day by day and do what I am supposed to do. I like to comb my hair and look at the mirror and beautify myself.

"I am getting ready to go out to the garden for a walk. The maid accompanies me. Out there is a small river ... it's just like in a little palace. I see other ladies like me and we greet each other and engage in a conversation. We are all nicely and elegantly dressed. All our husbands are back. We realize that we don't know exactly what is happening outside. There's fighting still ... the war ... the conversation is getting a bit serious.

"I get the feeling that my past life husband is Kent. He is engaged in some important discussion about war strategy. I am worried about the country and the safety of the people. Kent is walking back and forth in the study room thinking of a way out. He needs to make another journey out tomorrow. He has put on his gear and his armor. I give him a hug."

There was a sudden tone of insightful surprise.

"Oh ... now I understand why in the current life he always feels very comforted whenever I give him a hug! It is the same hug that I give him in the present life."

"How is the feeling now, as you are hugging him?"

"He feels sad in leaving me behind. (sobbing) He cannot bear to leave. I tell him to go and do what he is supposed to do. (sobbing) He hops onto the horse and leaves. I ask him to take care ... He has left already."

"How are you feeling now?"

"I feel alright. (sobbing) Here I am alone again, and doing my own stuff. Yeah, I can dance and play the musical string instrument. So when he is not around I can do all these things. Sometimes I do my calligraphy. I am a very refined lady and I have no children."

"Move on to the next significant event."

"Things are very chaotic now ... I see fires. People are killing each other from their horses ... with knives and swords .... There is a war going on."

"Where is your husband now?

"He is in the middle of the war ... Despite the chaos I am very steady and confident, and not in fear ... just a little worried. I am a lady with a lot of wisdom. A lot of people have died. I am waiting for my husband to come back."

"Is he back with you now?"

"Yes. He is tired ... not in a good shape. He has a lot of injuries ... cuts and bruises."

"What are your emotions at this stage?"

"I am a very strong lady and I do not shed a tear. I clean up his wounds, do the dressing and reassure him that everything will be fine. I give him a hug, and let him sleep."

"Does he say anything to you?"

"No. He does not tell me much about what happens in the war. He hardly talks ... keeps everything to himself ... all the sorrow and pain. It's like him in the present life. I feel very sad because I cannot help him even if I want to."

At the next event, Cindy saw herself in a pregnant state.

"My abdominal girth is increasing. I'm six months pregnant now. My husband is not at home ... Oh, I am about to deliver soon. He is back and waiting outside. A midwife delivers me. It is a baby boy ... my husband is happy. The boy is now two to three years old ... Kent is playing hide and seek with the boy. The boy is five to six years old now ...

"I think I am pregnant again. My husband is happy. The second baby is a girl ... The boy is very big now, eleven to twelve. Kent no longer goes to war ... he is more inbound, always busy with his work. The son adores him. He looks up to his father and observes every little single thing that he does. He tells me when he grows up he wants to be like his dad. I see at times Kent tells some stories, tales, and imparts some values to him. The girl sticks to me more often. Life is peaceful and good."

The regression ended at this point but the meaning behind this past life story was not immediately clear. Cindy asked for time to reflect over it herself.

The following morning at 7:00 am Cindy woke up with another insight. In her dreamy state of the mind, she gradually sensed the missing link. She told me that it was all about acceptance. Her life lesson was to accept and embrace the difference between the past and current lives. It was about accepting Kent as who he was in the present life and not forcing her expectations on him. They had both been frustrated and angry at each other because of their inability to accept each other's differences. She needed to learn to be independent of him from now onwards.

"I finally understood what my struggle is about. I don't like my current role because I expect my husband to be the provider for the family, just like in my past life. I feel uneasy to play the breadwinner role in this current life, even though I am capable and have enough resources. I guess that is because I am so used to the conducive and gentle way I play the typical supportive role in my past lives in ancient China. However, in the current life, I am forced to be more independent and take on a leading role. It is very tiring and I dislike this choice. Of course, the calling from within is to go that way. I can now see Kent's frustration. Despite that he has worked so hard, his achievements are meager. Well, with this, I have attained another level of understanding."

Session 9: Death and Rebirth

Cindy's emotions had stabilized. In the weeks that she had been undergoing therapy, Kent sensed a distinct change in her temperament. He noticed the increasing calmness within her and was puzzled. Somewhat uneasy with the distinct changes happening in her, he remained too preoccupied with his own career struggle to probe.

On Cindy's part, she no longer experienced turmoil with her relationship issue. However, she had become very intrigued with the bliss and harmony of her past life experience in ancient China. She came back on 21 November and wanted to explore her past life one step further.

She got into a trance state very fast this time, and it sounded like a continuation from where she had left during the last session.

"I see myself again in the same silk attire," Cindy said. "My son is quite big now. He is fifteen years old and quite a handsome, charming boy. He is wearing embroidered clothing with black shoes. He is sitting down and doing some reading and writing. I see a lot of Chinese words, paper and books. He is very intelligent and concentrating on his studies. His father is behind him, looking at the bookshelves. It is quite a serene environment. I am preparing tea and snacks for them. My daughter just walked in. She is about nine to ten years old and very bubbly and cheerful. She is disturbing her brother and asking him why is he studying so hard? The brother smiles and makes a facial gesture to indicate that their dad is behind them and to keep quiet."

The past life scene was filled with happiness. At the next event, Cindy saw herself at the death scene.

"I am lying on a bed. I am in my late fifties. Looks like I am sick. I have difficulty in breathing. My husband and my children are next to me. My daughter is in her twenties and is quite pretty. My husband is pacing to and fro. They are all worried and I think I am dying."

Cindy went into catharsis at this point.

"It is time for me to go. Kent just stares at me and as usual he does not know what to say. He is holding my hand," she said, sobbing away. "They all know it is my time to leave and feel sad. I am transiting quite peacefully ... I see myself floating ... I think I am out of my body. They are crying. I am now on the top of my body."

"What emotion do you feel at this stage?"

"Sadness. I cannot really let go. I am right in the clouds by myself now. I am lost in the white surroundings. I am asking myself: Where is this place?"

It appeared that Cindy arrived at the spirit realm. As she was figuring out her whereabouts, I guided her to meet up with her spirit guide.

"Yeah, an old man appeared and I am looking up at him. He is quite a big-sized male with shoulder-length hair. He carries a wooden staff with something hanging from the top. I ask him for guidance on my life purpose."

"What does your spirit guide say?"

There was a pause and Cindy sounded perplexed.

"He says I am free to choose ... and go with my heart."

Catharsis was setting in at this point.

"He says I have a very good heart and am very well protected (crying) and I will always be protected. But, I am not sure how to choose! I ask him for advice. He says I will know. He also tells me to trust my instinct and use my wisdom and there's nothing to be afraid of."

I later realized that these words were stuck in Cindy's mind for several months thereafter.

"Ask him what is your purpose in this life that has just ended."

"He says it has to do with love. I need to know what is love, and then how to let go of it."

Suddenly, I noticed a change in Cindy's tone.

"Oh ... I see a tunnel, and I am inside it! At the end of the tunnel is a very bright light. I am walking towards the light. It is getting brighter and brighter. As I walk towards the end of the tunnel I realize that the light is white. It seems like I am going to another plane."

The description of the dark tunnel and "white light" had all the features consistent with a near-death (NDE) experience.[2] In spirituality, the white light is considered a divine, healing light. It is the space in the universe where positive energies are stored. When the white light is encountered in an NDE it is believed to be a manifestation of one's Higher Self, and is usually accompanied by feelings of peacefulness and bliss.

There was a pause as Cindy was experiencing herself in this different realm.

"An image is appearing at the end of the tunnel. It's like going to another place and I don't know what it's going to be like. Oh! ... I am through to another place now ... I see a baby."

"Describe the baby to me."

"He is wrapped in a white cloth and is near the arms of the mother."

Suddenly Cindy had a revelation. "Oh ... I am the baby! I am a very healthy baby and feel good ... kicking, moving, and

---

[2] The core-NDE experience was described by Kenneth Ring, an eminent researcher in the 1970s and 1980s.

smiling. I have very nice-looking eyes. The baby's mother is carrying her."

Next moment, Cindy acquired a further insight. "I have a sense that the mother is my mother in this current life." She broke into catharsis again at this point.

"How do you feel when you find that it is your own mother?"

"I feel safe. (voice wavering) Her love towards me is very strong."

"What is the message you learn from this love?"

"It is about giving ... giving freely, and learning how to be a woman, providing the warmth whenever it is needed." There was a sense of ecstatic delight in her statement.

"Do you see a pattern that is related to your present life?"

"Yes, I now know how to understand, how to be simple and to detect others' feelings ... it comes from the heart and willingly." Cindy's voice turned dreamy at this point. "I can learn from Mum how to give. She has so much to give and never asks for anything in return."

The session ended with an air of finale. The feeling was that of peace and bliss, very much akin to a classical NDE.

Only seven weeks ago, Cindy was emotionally labile, but now with her shift in consciousness, she calmly sought my consensus to end her therapy at this point because she wanted to move on independently. She had been through a tough healing journey and learned a valuable lesson through surviving it. She had since understood Kent a lot better. What was remarkable was her development of awareness of her deeper levels of being and the ability to see beyond her limitations. Most important of all, she was now able to love Kent differently, and from a distance.

On 22 January 2013, I heard that there was a significant change of heart with Kent. It was just before the Chinese New Year holiday period. Kent had decided to hold back his decision to move out of the house. On 10 February Cindy and Kent arranged for a family holiday and went to Malaysia with their two children. It was a memorable occasion. They drove across the Woodlands Causeway and headed towards Port Dickson. The weather was fantastic and the traffic was light during the holiday season. It was a most relaxing and lovely time that they spent bonding with the children.

"As I am reflecting now, I realize this is the first time that Kent and I have had such a peaceful trip," Cindy recalled. "I have now learned to let go and not force my wants on him. I sat at the beach with him looking out to the sea and feeling peaceful and serene as always …"

It sounded almost like a miracle coming true. Unfortunately, a month later, something triggered another change in Kent's mind. Once again, he wanted to move out of the house. It was very painful news for Cindy who had, all this while, been making a tremendous effort to save the marriage.

Unsure of what was going on in Kent's mind, Cindy handled the situation firmly and very differently from her previous self. She accepted his decision without question. She then looked for another apartment to stay and moved out of the house with the children before Kent did.

Kent was taken aback. He felt uneasy with her firm and sudden move and regretted his action. He offered to reverse his decision and pleaded with Cindy to move back to the house and have a fresh start with their marriage. However, Cindy was steadfast. She was clear that she needed the emotional space for herself. She felt they could still work on their marriage issues even in the separation stage.

From her emotional wounds, Cindy had developed a scar which was telling the story that she had survived her healing journey. She understood that she had been using her marriage relationship, all this while, as a crutch to lean on. Now she had discovered that the crutches no longer fit her needs and were too painful to wear.

Eventually Kent accepted what she had done and agreed to come up with a list of activities for the family and children as part of his commitment to continue to work on the marriage. As I heard the news, I was reminded of a saying from Neale Donald Walsch:

"Life begins at the end of your comfort zone. So if you're feeling uncomfortable right now, know that the change taking place in your life is a beginning, not an ending."

Cindy explained her action to me calmly. "I have now taken a wait-and-see position in terms of my relationship with Kent. While my heart is still open for him, I am reassessing the needs of myself, my children, and my husband in a broader perspective. It's a neutral approach I am taking this time. Basically, I am relinquishing my control on him and letting him be free. He needs to be truthful to himself and be sure of what he wants in our relationship and how he wants to run his life."

Time passed. I checked with Cindy some months later as to how she was progressing in her life.

"I am actually doing very well. Not to worry," she reassured me. "I am currently swamped by my office work and I stay back late regularly. Not sure if it is a good thing but it definitely shifted my concentration away from my personal issues with Kent. It has been more than three months living in separation and my attachment to him has decreased dramatically.

"I have learned a lot about positive affirmations, which is so powerful about changing negative thoughts. Healing is really about self-care and self-manifestation."

I was pleasantly surprised with her progress.

"When I reflect back on my life, I did unconsciously manifest what I have. I have always wished to have two kids and be a working mum in a high-rise office and drawing a comfortable income. All these are happening now," Cindy explained.

"The separation has in fact served me well and allowed me the space to reassess the whole situation and figure out what is it that I actually want. It lifts the pressure off us. There are no longer any quarrels or disagreement, and there are no more arguments and shouting. We are both free, and no longer controlling each other. This paves the way for me to decide on the life I want to live."

I was impressed. Cindy appeared to have learned to trust whatever she was dealing with. Whatever doorway to crisis she experienced was leading her to a greater lesson in living where the power of love was at work.

A further two months passed and I heard from Cindy again. It was 17 June, and her message started with: "I have finally found the truth about my life purpose."

This immediately captured my attention, and I read on:

"You remember during my last regression session I asked my spirit guide what am I supposed to do? The voice said to me that I can choose what I want. I was perplexed then. Well, I have just understood that my purpose is what I say it is, and my mission is the mission I give myself."

As I read her message, my eyes were fixed on it with amazement. I saw freedom and beauty in her mind. It took my breath away as I was hypnotized by the wonder of the change that had taken place in her.

"My life purpose will be to create myself and create who I really am. I have just realized that I had always been asking for other people's approval for what I do. The truth is that I am the one dictating how my life is going to be, not other people. I am here to express and fulfill who I really am."

That was a most exhilarating moment; it extruded a feeling that words could not describe. Cindy's search for her life purpose had been tough. As I stood by her side throughout her journey of change, I had sensed a spurt of spiritual growth in myself. It was like a self-transformation after having made a difference to someone's life.

PART TWO

Love and Relationships

CHAPTER THREE

Inner Child Healing in Strained Relationships

Dr. Soumya Rao P.

"When I talk to you, whom am I addressing? The Inner Child, seeking so hopefully for some sign that it is loved? Or the Teenager, buttressed against an unfriendly world, searching desperately for the truth? Or is it the Adult Intellect, struggling so hard to hold everything together? Let me speak to your Soul wandering through space like a castaway, caught up in a psychophysiological trap created by eons of suffering, the imprisoned splendor of this remote planet."

Ernest Pecci

Being brought up in a traditional Indian household by a disciplinarian father and a God-fearing mother, I have been introduced to spirituality at a very early stage in my life. This includes the concepts of karma and reincarnation as part of the Hindu belief system. Furthermore, I have also befriended a homeopath neighbor who believes in self-healing and he shares with me his books on energy work and natural remedies.

While I enjoyed my medical undergraduate days and the knowledge gained, I have been a little disillusioned with the fact that the root causes of many medical illnesses remain unidentified. After graduation, I choose to pursue a career in mental health because I strongly believe that our thoughts and feelings are important contributors to health and disease. For four years I stayed in the United Kingdom undergoing postgraduate training in Psychiatry, and it was at this point of time that I stumbled upon Dr. Brian Weiss' bestseller on past life regression.[3] This opened up a new path for me. The concepts described in his books provided me with answers to many of my existential questions, and have indirectly shaped my career. Henceforth, I knew exactly what my life goal was. After qualifying as a psychiatrist, I obtained my training in regression therapy from the Life Research Academy[4], Hyderabad, India, and have since dedicated myself to a lifetime's search for the tools of self-transformation and healing.

My Journey as Therapist
In the course of my journey, I realized that it is common for us to ignore our emotional wellbeing in the midst of our busy life routines. We brush problems under the carpet to carry on with our lives. Often, we distract ourselves from festering wounds of the past, thinking that they will go away with time.

For some of us, we tend to let ourselves be ruled by incomprehensible fears and irrational beliefs. For many others, we battle our lack of self-worth and confidence, struggling to find

---

[3] Dr. Brian Weiss is Chairman Emeritus of Psychiatry in the Mt. Sinai Medical Center of Miami, USA. He is the author of *Many Lives, Many Masters* and is a medical pioneer in past life regression.
[4] The Life Research Academy is founded by Dr. Newton for the training of past life regression therapy in India.

out how and where these fears have sprung from. In the process, we have to confront our inner anger and impulsive outbursts. Added to this is our perennial relationship with guilt, which limits us from living our lives to the fullest.

How then do we address these tribulations of life? The answer, I believe, lies in our willingness to confront them. We begin by saying "Hello" to the pain within, knowing that it has been bothering us for a long time, and making an effort to talk about it. This is the first step.

It is well known that the way we feel, think and behave is heavily influenced by our upbringing. What we have been told and what has been done to us when we were children have shaped our psyche. Many of us can consciously remember how certain mishaps or events in our childhood have impacted our behavior and personality. However, some children repress memories that are traumatic, as if those things had never happened to them. Consequently, the ghost of our past continues to haunt us in many ways and baffles us, as adults.

As humans living on this planet, we expect to live in ideal homes with flawless parents, perfect childhoods and wonderful opportunities ahead of us. The reality is that none of us are blessed with all these gifts. We grow up dealing with our disillusionment, either by denying that our childhood has been unhappy and fraught with inadequate parenting, or by remaining angry with all that has happened to us. Most children are loved conditionally. They are accepted only when they meet parental expectations. They grow up having trouble accepting themselves the way they are. As children are unable to see things the way adults do, they tend to develop distorted perceptions about themselves and their lives as adults.

Child Abuse

Children identify with their feelings as part of themselves. All that children want is to be accepted for who they are and as individuals with minds of their own. When their feelings are judged, they feel as if they are being evaluated as good or bad individuals. These feelings remain buried deep in their subconscious mind and persist to surface as a disturbing influence in later life. When they grow up as adults, they forget all about their inner child as they fall prey to the travails of human life.

Time and again, the inner child in the form of a sub-personality shows up in different life situations and pretty much

succeeds in putting the adult intellect into conflict. Despite our ability to connect all the dots back in time, it still does not stop us from experiencing the old pain, however aware we are of the reason and the time it happened.

For a better and brighter future for everyone, we are collectively responsible for providing a non-judgmental and an unconditionally loving space for children to grow up and become empowered citizens of the world. What is commonly encountered in clinical practice is child abuse of a physical, emotional and sexual nature. It is deemed that sheer physical and emotional neglect of a child also amounts to abuse, because it poses a serious threat to one's integrity and scars the individual for life.

"Even with the spotlight of publicity on child abuse today, confusion and misunderstanding reign regarding its occurrence. Hostility and hatred of children exist in our culture and other cultures as well, and the prevalence of

abuse and the enormity of its effects are still not recognized. A large segment of people still believe that child abuse is insignificant and are convinced that children lie about and exaggerate such abuse."

Alice Givens

The concepts of omission and commission are relevant here. The act of omission covers a child's needs during upbringings that are either inadequately given or not done at all. Examples are providing inadequate food, poor shelter and lack of physical care or emotional nurture. On the other hand, the act of commission covers the things that should not be done, but have been meted out to the vulnerable and powerless child. This includes all forms and degrees of physical, emotional and sexual trauma.

In most households, children are abused in varying degrees for doing all the normal things, such as being curious and inquisitive, speaking loudly and screaming in excitement, being clumsy and creating chaos, asking for what they want, soiling their clothes, wanting to play all the time, asking questions and speaking their mind to the adults, etc. Abuse of their rights and needs and not valuing their authenticity makes them grow up irrationally defensive about their selves, wanting to protect themselves from the world and not allow anyone into their personal space.

Physical and verbal abuse is rampant across cultures based on the belief that it is a necessary evil to discipline children. However, it creates a paralyzing fear and pushes the vulnerable children almost immediately into an altered state, registering the fear complex deeply. Since verbal and physical abuse are often associated, these children grow up to be adults believing that the adjectives that have been used on them, such as "worthless", "evil", "bad", "ugly", and "useless", are true.

A lack of acknowledgment and appreciation of the little individual in the family, as if his opinions do not matter, can contribute to poor self-worth, a lack of a voice and a feeling of being permanently trapped in a cocoon of his own.

Emotional abuse is common in all households. When deprecating words are spoken in association with an emotional charge, it is just as detrimental even in the absence of physical trauma. A dire psycho-socio-economic status in a family can perpetrate severe emotional neglect, lack of affection, generous criticism, negative judgments and the use of verbal obscenities towards children. This creates a childhood environment of depression, hopelessness and helplessness that may reflect in adulthood as neurosis that requires psychiatric treatment.

Sexual abuse, on the other hand, is even more complex. It is rarely talked about, and is often concealed by both the victim and abuser. Families continue to live cheerfully, as if sexual abuse does not happen or does not exist. It is true that abusers are usually either family members or friends in close social circles with access to vulnerable children, rather than strangers. The childhood experience is usually repressed and forgotten, but it remains deeply knotted and buried in the subconscious. There is always a distorted relationship between the abuser and the victim, in which the latter is invariably made to feel guilty by the former. The victim is often made to believe he should do nothing to stop the process, because he derives some pleasure from it, and that he is someone special who is being loved dearly. This coerces him into swearing secrecy.

The symptomatology of sexual abuse consists of a vague fear, irrational anger, poor sense of self-worth, disturbed body image and difficulties with relationships and intimacy. It takes an unconditional and non-judgmental therapist to guide a victim into disentangling these knots gradually, and at the patient's own pace.

Fundamentally, a child needs physical warmth and affection as an expression of unconditional love from a parent. A gentle, affectionate embrace from his loved one goes a long way in making him feel secure and comfortable. However, in some cultures it is considered shameful to show love as a physical gesture. It is as if love is automatically conveyed and understood by a child somehow without being demonstrated to him.

Healing the Child Within

When a child is attacked by external trauma, the experience leads to defensive freezing in the interest of survival. For healing to take place, the frozen energies such as fear, anger, abuse, humiliation, hopelessness and neglect must be released from the memories of the past events. Creating a safe and trusting space, where a patient can let go of resistance and express the old pains from childhood, followed by a reframing of the situation, is the start of a good session. A therapist, who has worked on his own deeper issues with transformational learning and self-acceptance, can then help patients on their healing journey.

"... be in touch with your feelings, begin to be in touch with the part of you that you need to look at. Because there is a part of you that really yearns for understanding, for reconciliation, for a broadening of awareness ... begin to see a shift now, a shift in seeing."

Ronald Wong Jue

The inner child is essentially that part of the individual's psyche that derives energy from both fear- and love-based memories conceptualized during childhood. These emotions are registered in the subconscious mind and react autonomously to life situations. Inner child therapy provides an opportunity for the patient to accept the child within unconditionally, and reframe childhood memories to get on to the path of healing.

Therapy begins by inducing the patient into a hypnotic or an altered state of consciousness. The patient is then is guided to relive a childhood memory which may be responsible for a particular problem in his life. The experience is re-evaluated from the child's perspective, and then juxtaposed with the mature understanding of the adult. It is usually done by engaging the patient in a meaningful dialogue under trance until a conflict is resolved.

As part of the therapy process, it helps to make use of mythological and fantasy characters, like super-heroes, demi-gods or any known powerful entity from our childhood experience, including power animals[5], to leverage on their energies while reframing the inner child experience. This approach is both empowering and transformational in releasing emotional trauma.

In a nutshell, the inner child refers to the sum total of all the mental-emotional energies stored in the subconscious mind of the child from birth to puberty. Inner child therapy works by integrating the various sub-personalities[6] of one's psyche, namely the child, the adult and the parent "parts", to make the individual feel whole.

---

[5] A power animal is an animistic and shamanic concept of a tutelary spirit that protects the individual from harm and lends the wisdom or attributes of the particular animal to the individual under its protection.
[6] A sub-personality is a particular thought, feeling or action mode that kicks in to cope with certain types of situations

A Bridge to Past Lives

Childhood memories of pain and trauma can also carry energies over from past life trauma which may be reactivated by a similar experience in the current life. Inner child therapy facilitates the patient to identify such patterns from past lives in which he is trapped. It is useful as a springboard to access the relevant past lives where the pattern originated.

If we look at trauma in the "one-life-only" school of thought, the use of inner child therapy for treatment of emotional trauma can mitigate the severity of symptoms, lighten up the personality and allow the patient to see it as a trough in the wave of his current life experience.

When the trauma is viewed in the extended perspective of past lives, the soul is seen as being on a continuing journey to experience various emotional polarities and integrate this learning for its own spiritual evolution and acquisition of wisdom.

> *"Life is like a string of pearls, the self being the thread and the pearls side by side are life experiences, births and deaths being a continuum, all opportunities for growth in consciousness."*
>
> *Barbara Findeisen*

In the following section I am illustrating the process of inner child therapy with a narration of the therapy sessions of two of my patients who have since undergone transformational changes.

While many approaches are available with this mode of therapy, I use hypnotic regression primarily in my practice. This is because working in altered states of consciousness with guided imagery facilitates the process of reframing childhood stories. The aim is to achieve a positive cognitive restructuring of their beliefs along with a change in their bioenergy fields. Where appropriate, I use body therapy[7] and breathwork[8] to release frozen energies from their memories. The change in the voice, body language, and demeanor during the session and at follow-up visits is a validation of what they have processed internally, during and after the therapy.

THE CASE OF NALINI – CHILD ABUSE

Nalini walked into my clinic one day looking very disturbed and was desperate for help. She had a dejected appearance and was brimming to pour out her sorrow. Tears flowed as she began to narrate her saga.

Nalini was thirty-five years old, slightly overweight, married and living with her husband and in-laws. She previously worked as an accountant but was now staying at home looking after a two-year-old son. Her main concern was her strained relationship with her husband. It all stemmed from an incompatible sexual relationship after their marriage. Her husband was dominating, sexually aggressive and wanted his fantasies fulfilled, and at the same time vociferous about his disappointments. Nalini, on the other hand, was suffering from a poor body image and a low sex drive. She was unable to fulfill her husband's needs and had difficulty reciprocating his sexual advances. She had hoped for a loving companion who could be more tender and sensitive to her needs but was disappointed. She felt rejected, bullied and guilty for failing to satisfy her husband. Under pressure to be a "perfect" partner, her self-worth went right down.

---

[7] Body therapy is a branch of psychotherapy that applies the principles of somatic psychology as developed by Wilhelm Reich.
[8] Breathwork refers to various forms of alteration of conscious breathing that are used within psychotherapy or meditation.

In the course of our discussion, I realized that she had always put other people's interests ahead of her own. She did not know how to say "no" to others and had tried hard to please others so that she could be appreciated and loved. However, when they did not reciprocate, a sense of rejection and guilt set in. Clearly, she had lost her sense of self.

Nalini recounted two failed relationships in the past. One was a six-year-long relationship during her college days that ended sadly, because the guy couldn't commit to marriage. As a rebound to the break-up, she subsequently had an affair with a work colleague which turned rather sore. It was clear that, in both instances, she had attracted abusive men. They initially seemed very loving but both were domineering beneath the surface. Unsuspectingly, she assumed the role of a pleasing and hapless victim.

From her clinical history, Nalini sounded as if she was stuck in a pattern of abusive relationships. She confided in me that she felt like she was mixed up in a bag of negative emotions that ranged from oppression and anger to sadness and powerlessness. She was aware of how people exploited her kindness, but it was uncanny how she always attracted such people into her life. Exhausted through carrying out responsibilities that were not hers, and never making time for herself, her physical health had suffered. She suffered from frequent throat infections and her chronic asthma was exacerbated during stressful periods.

Nalini was the second child in a family of two, with an elder brother. Her mother favored the son but she was her father's princess. She grew up with the feeling that her mother had neglected her, and felt insecure. She sketchily recalled a few episodes of sexual abuse when she was around eight years of age.

She was very fond of her father, who was a busy man in a transferable job. She had spent many years of her childhood longing for him. He was staying in different cities in the course of his work, and would occasionally come home to visit her during holidays. The mother and children were staying put in one place as a base for the children's education. She shared a cordial but emotionally distant relationship with her brother, who was five years her senior. Nalini remembered feeling lonely at home and not having her mother's affection as she doted more on her son.

Nalini was deeply troubled by her victim consciousness that was brought about by a childhood blatantly crying of insecurity, emotional starvation, mistrust and sexual abuse. These emotions had spilled over into her present moment. After thinking through her problem I offered regression therapy. She accepted the offer although she understood that it could be a long road to healing.

Regression 1: At the Temple

After a hypnotic induction that involved a breathing exercise and progressive relaxation, Nalini went into an altered state of consciousness. I brought her memory back to the event that involved sexual abuse.

"I am with my mother, on my way to a temple. I don't like to go there," she began. "My mum is dragging me along and telling me that God will be angry with me if I don't go. My heart is racing."

Nalini was beginning to look restless. She had earlier given me a past history of unexplained palpitations, and she looked as if another attack was about to come on.

"I am feeling weak in my legs. I don't feel good. Something is about to happen ... I don't like the feeling." There was fear in her voice. At this point I guided her to breathe deeply and stay connected to her feelings, intensifying them with each breath. It was a body-centered approach to therapy that I took.

In a body therapy, it is assumed that the body holds back echoes of early shocks and trauma. These can be released if the therapist allows the patient's unexpressed emotions to complete their responses. Central to this approach is the "body-mind" concept that recognizes that each individual is a unity consisting of both a body and a mind that are inseparable and intertwined. A generated emotion is understood as simultaneously both a psychological and a physiological event. Emotional memories appear as feelings and persist in the course of the patient's life. It is the intrinsic nature of feelings to express themselves somatically and anything that interrupts this expression is problematic.

Soon Nalini began to feel a pang of fear in her chest. This pain seemed to represent an undischarged feeling held in the form of muscular tension in her chest.

"I can't breathe anymore. I feel something is on my chest ... it's huge. Oh, it's heavy ... I can feel a hand on my mouth! I want to scream but I can't."

Nalini was sobbing heavily, as the memory of her childhood abuse gradually emerged.

"I feel hurt down there ... something is poking me very deeply ... I can't see anything, I feel blind ... Oh my God!"

Nalini was crying intensely as she was reliving the scene of trauma with a feeling of total powerlessness.

I continued to guide her to stay in the body to relive the experience until it was over. It was difficult. She struggled to stay connected with the imagery and I suggested that she ask her Higher Self to allow her to visualize what had happened. Eventually she gathered enough courage to go through the experience.

"I can see him now. He is so huge, scary and dark. He is closing my mouth so that I can't scream. He puts his fingers into me ... down there, and it hurts so much!"

Nalini was in tears.

"He is pinning me against the wall and pressing his arm on my chest. Oh God, I am going to die!" After a long, deep breath Nalini started to struggle.

"He is telling me to touch his *wee wee,* and thereafter he forces it into my mouth!"

It was disgusting. Nalini coughed violently. She struggled to breathe and experienced a nauseated and choking feeling. She indicated that she wanted to end the session at this point, because it was emotionally too heavy.

I empathized and brought her back to the here and now. However, we mutually agreed that we would resume the therapy another time. It took her a while before she accepted that the event actually took place. We discussed and decided that we could perhaps work through her trauma in stages.

Regression 2: Power Animal

In the next session we revisited the same scene at the temple. This time Nalini was more prepared to face the trauma, having spent a good deal of time reflecting on it. Back to that same memory under trance, I facilitated her to re-experience the event as an observer rather than as a participant in the process. This made it easier for her to stay engaged.

She now recognized the abuser as a priest and one of the temple officials, who was well known to the family. He had befriended her when she visited the temple with her parents. She could sense that something about him had made her uneasy even as a little girl, but couldn't say what. He appeared very kind and had lured her into a small room at the temple while her mother was observing the religious rituals.

"He was waving at me, and said he had a surprise for me. He gave me a toffee. After I ate it, he began to undress me and himself." Nalini began to cry loudly.

"I knew it felt so wrong, but I didn't know what to do. I shouldn't have gone in. He spoke sweet things to me many times and it all happened so quickly. He said it was our special friendship and no one is supposed to know about this ... and good girls don't refuse anything that they are asked to do."

Nalini continued to cry uncontrollably. The unsuspecting child had walked into a hell-hole and back while the rest of the crowd, including her mother, was staying engrossed in a religious ritual.

At this point, Nalini spontaneously connected with her body, and thoroughly experienced the disgust and shame of the trauma of oral sex being forced on her. It left her feeling dirty, nauseated and ashamed of her own body. She became hard to console and it took her some time to get over it.

"My mother is so lost; she doesn't even know I am missing!" she said bitterly. "Her attention is focused on the temple idol, and I just went to him. I should have stayed, and should have said 'no' to him ... but I can't say no! ... I just can't say no!" Nalini was sobbing away.

"How can she be so careless? No one knows that this is happening to me!"

Nalini's feelings were a mix of guilt and anger and it left her in deep conflict.

"I am so angry right now. I wish I could kill him!"

Nalini was feeling furious inside, and was breathing heavily. I also noted that her fists were clenched. Immediately, I encouraged her to intensify these feelings, and use her body to fully express her repressed anger and release the frozen energy. I positioned a pillow for her to pounce her fists on. At the same time, I decided to infuse the strength of a power animal into her body so she would feel strong enough to "punish" the abuser.

"Dear body, what power animal do you wish to have now, that which you didn't have the last time?"

"I am connecting to a lioness which protects her cub from danger." After a pause she said, "Yes ... I am receiving her strength now."

Nalini stretched her arms and legs as she was experiencing the new feeling and power of a lioness. "I am feeling strong now. I am pouncing on him ... tearing his body apart ... and digging my claws into his body. He is writhing in pain. My cub is behind me watching."

The mention of the word "cub" was pertinent as it was a signification of her inner child in this context. Nalini breathed deeply and heavily after she let out her anger. This was followed by a long pause.

"He is wounded badly. He dares not touch my cub anymore. He is dead. I have killed him. That crook is dead. I feel more peaceful now."

The use of a power animal was one way in which the parent-self in her could be facilitated to take charge of protecting her inner child by reframing the whole scene into one with transformed power.

"It's not your fault ... you are my little innocent child! I am so sorry you have to go through this. You are safe now as I am here. I am with you always. You are pure and divine ... nothing can touch you. You are my little angel ... hold on to me."

Nalini was tightly embracing and holding on to a stuffed doll that symbolically represented her inner child. She wept tears of relief. After her throat relaxed, she found it easier to talk.

Within the same therapy session, we revisited this traumatic memory a few more times until she had released all residual emotion. In her altered state of consciousness, she recalled that her abuser had ogled her every time she visited the temple. He had touched her inappropriately several times and kissed her on her lips. The eight-year-old girl knew it didn't feel right but was unable to communicate this feeling to her mother then. He had sworn her to secrecy by saying it was their special friendship.

Her inability to say no to people stemmed from the distorted belief that she couldn't refuse anyone because "good girls don't say no". The paralyzing fear of her abuser who talked her into the distorted belief was now evident. She now understood how the feeling of powerlessness she had been experiencing sexually with her husband and previous partners had stemmed from the childhood abuse. She began to understand how the complexities of sexual abuse generated the guilt in her. By engaging her adult and parent selves in a voice dialogue with her inner child she was able to work on her guilt and self-deprecating beliefs slowly and steadily.

Nalini's journey of healing had begun. The sessions were cathartic, but she successfully unearthed all the repressed anger and guilt she experienced as an eight-year-old child and had since transformed herself.

Regression 3: Healing Light
A month later during a follow-up visit, I saw that Nalini was emotionally less strung and more confident in herself. Her body language told me she was more relaxed. She reported feeling a huge load off her chest and she had been practicing the act of saying no consciously whenever she wanted to. It still needed effort but she could do it now. Her throat felt better and her asthmatic attacks were less frequent.

Under trance, she returned readily back to the same event but feeling more at ease this time, having undergone significant catharsis in her earlier sessions. She was focusing more on how she felt towards her mother's indifference in this session.

"My mother forces me to go to the temple with her and I don't like it," she recalled. "I am angry with her for being careless. How can she not know what was going on? She is my mother and none of this would have happened if she had noticed and protected me." She was sobbing again.

This time I initiated healing by guiding her to visualize herself, her inner child and her mother to be seated in a huge ball of healing light. Her inner child was encouraged to express her anguish towards the mother for not protecting her. She voiced her feelings loud and clear until she was done. The mother figure begged for forgiveness profusely and embraced the child.

This was a transformational moment. Subsequently, Nalini was able to revisit the memory more dispassionately and understand her mother's plight.

"My mother was disappointed with her life. She was lonely too. She missed my father, who was not around to share her responsibilities. She was exhausted. Whenever she was at the temple, she would tend to forget her worries. I could see why she was preoccupied. She trusted the man and didn't bother when he took me away for a while. I can forgive her now. She tried her best and it was too much on her."

Regression 4: Gender Bias

Nalini had other issues to address. She came for another therapy session to work on her feelings of being rejected by her mother, and its impact on her adult-self.

Once under trance, she was brought to a scene where she saw her mother was holding her brother in embrace and admiring his good looks.

"She says he is so much fairer than I am." Nalini spoke with a sad tone. "She is cuddling him and stroking his head. She thinks I am not as beautiful as she has expected, and is worried if I can be easily married off when I grow up."

Nalini was very upset.

"I am feeling lonely and rejected. I can't understand why Mum favors him over me. I am ugly. She never hugs me like the way she hugs him." Nalini started to weep.

"I want her to love me, but she doesn't ... she thinks I am a burden to her." It was Nalini's adult-self talking. "My mother feels that a daughter will get married and leave, whereas her son is her only solace. She believes that her son is going to take care of her when she grows old. She loves him more than she loves me."

Catharsis set in. Nalini turned emotional and cried. I waited till she felt more relieved.

"I want to make my mother happy. I have tried but nothing makes her smile; nothing seems to take her attention away from my brother. He is always the favored child. I am missing my dad."

There was a long pause as she continued to weep.

"Dad would have taken care of me. He loves me dearly." Nalini understood that her urge to please everyone, especially her mother, was related to this event. If she couldn't make somebody happy, it would constitute a failure on her part. She could see the origin of her distorted assumptions had come from her childhood and was able to reframe the experience.

Without suggestion from me, she allowed the archetype of the loving parent in her to take over, embracing the little Nalini with unconditional love.

Next, adult Nalini started to speak to the child version of herself. "It is absolutely perfect to be a girl," she said to her younger self. "Girls are wonderful, and you are wonderful, my dear child! I love you and will always be there for you. You bring joy to me."

Nalini repeated the affirmations several times in her altered state, until the energy of the session transformed and her inner child felt secure.

Nalini was now able to understand that the underlying feeling of sadness and rejection as an adult was rooted in her affection-deprived childhood. She also realized she had been unconsciously seeking this lost affection in all her adult relationships.

To enhance the healing, Nalini was connected back to happy memories in her subsequent therapy sessions. The aim was to derive more strength from these memories and bring hope back to her life to reinforce positivity. I guided her to connect with some beautiful memories she had spent as a child, in the company of her father. Indeed, there were instances of family travel and holidays together where she was pampered by him. She was spoiled and provided with lots of gifts and sweets whenever the father was back home. She missed him terribly whenever he was away for months. However, she was able to reinforce the parent-self with the image of her father who loved her and treated her well. She consciously visualized memories of herself with her father as a regular practice to feel the love and worthiness he had given her.

The inner child therapy sessions had made a significant difference between the way Nalini had earlier viewed her life and now. For one, she had realized the impact of those events on her personality. She started making conscious efforts to look after herself and practiced positive affirmations and assertiveness. She was much more in control of her emotions and had improved her communication with her husband by voicing her needs.

THE CASE OF ROHAN – CHILD NEGLECT

Rohan was a thirty-year-old, lean, tall, handsome man who had been married for three years and worked as an IT professional. His wife was working in the same industry. Although he had a good marriage, he wanted to address some of his fears and limitations, which had recently begun to have a bearing on his married life.

Rohan came with the complaint of "feeling stuck" in his life both professionally and personally. He experienced an inability to progress in his life and a lack of motivation to change. He was fully aware that one of part of him wanted to change whereas another part of him was not prepared to work for it.

First and foremost, he had problems of intimacy with his wife, and felt particularly uncomfortable when it involved physical affection. Funnily, he felt awkward even when he received hugs from her, and whenever her arms were around his shoulders. Even the act of cuddling up to his wife needed a significant effort on his part. He believed that he fell short in reciprocating love to his wife because of his physical awkwardness.

Financially, Rohan was contented with his income and never aspired for more, although he admitted that he had the earning potential; nor did he take any big risks at work or in his personal life. He was happy with a bike as his mode of transport even though he felt his family could enjoy more if they had a car. He lived in a rented house although he was capable of owning one. He never enjoyed shopping for things for himself but he loved to spend on his wife. His laidback attitude and lack of drive to achieve bigger things in life was worrying him.

In our initial conversation, I discovered that he had been spending very little throughout his childhood. He did not have many toys or much clothing; nor did he demand more from his parents. His mum always did the shopping for him and his brother. He remembered feeling adequately provided for and never complained about scarcity. He claimed to have had a reasonably happy childhood, without any history of trauma or abuse.

Regression 1: At Six Months and Five Years

After the initial assessment, Rohan agreed to undergo hypnotherapy. Once under trance, I used an age regression approach with the aim of understanding those memories and beliefs from his early childhood that could have influenced him.

We started by going back to a very early age of his life. After an initial breathing and relaxation exercise, he slipped into a moderately deep trance and immediately connected with a childhood event at the age of six months. He saw himself in his mother's lap and was breast-feeding. His mother was indifferent, and appeared preoccupied with other thoughts during the feeding process, while he was restless and hungry for attention.

"I can feel my mother's physical presence, but she is not connected to me emotionally. She just wants to feed me and be done with it. It's another routine job," Rohan said bitterly as his inner child was crying out for the mother's attention during the feeding.

"She is mulling over a fight she had with my father. She is not enjoying the moment, and I don't feel any love from her. I am feeding because I am hungry, and I am not enjoying it either." He realized he was being deprived of his mother's emotional attention.

"I want my mother to sing and stroke me when she feeds me, and to say some nice things to me. She is busy, worried and angry, and as always her mind is somewhere else. I am missing her touch. She is so indifferent. I don't want her milk."

Rohan started to weep. He then recollected similar memories when he was about two years old, while his mother was dressing him up but devoid of any kind words, cuddle or kiss. He felt emotionally starved and had deeply longed for his mother's warm loving touch in vain. There were instances where he ran up to her, wanting an embrace, but was pushed away because she was busy with household chores. He recognized how much he longed for the warmth as a child, the very thing he was denying himself and his wife at the moment.

At this point, I encouraged Rohan to connect deeply with his feelings in the body. He was in tears as he expressed his need to be held, embraced and loved. He was angry with his mother for being indifferent and preoccupied. I then guided him to reframe the memory into the way he wanted it, using body work to express his anger. Part of this involved encouraging him to use his fists and leg movements, while under trance, to throw a tantrum at his mother. He was able to draw his mother's affection by howling and verbally demanding that she love him.

What followed was a visual imagery of him in his mother's arms immersed in unconditional love. He was given a soft toy, which represented his inner child, to hold in loving embrace.

"What is it that you want to happen now, that didn't happen previously?" I asked.

"I want my mother to express her affection to me," Rohan replied. A moment later he visualized changes in the imagery.

"I am crying and howling now. I have stopped feeding and I want her attention. She is wondering why I am howling and is beginning to rock me. She is now talking to me, with sweet loving words. She lifts me up, holding me in embrace and stroking me. She is worried about what went wrong, and I am slowly feeling better. She is more caring and is talking to me now. She sings a lullaby, strokes me, puts me in bed and stays next to me. I calm down and continue feeding till I am done. She is gently rocking to put me to sleep and I am feeling good. I can see that my mother has a smile and is satisfied too."

A sense of relief just spread over his otherwise stiff demeanor and this was followed by a smile, resulting from having finally experienced the ecstasy of the mother's touch. He was allowed to revel in this beautiful moment for a long while.

Moving him on to an older age hypnotically, Rohan connected with another past event where he had fallen down accidentally while playing. He was about five years old and he recalled being injured.

"My knees are wounded. I have fallen down while playing and I am crying. My mother comes out of the house. She is angry with me and is scolding me for being careless. She drags me inside the house, and is hitting me on my buttocks for being careless!

"How can she be angry with me? I am so hurt. I want her to be nice to me. She is now putting some lotion on the wound. Aargh! It burns and makes me feel worse. Why can't she be kind to me? I am so angry with her. She never plays with me, and now she is upset and shouting at me. I don't like this." Rohan started to weep as he spoke.

"I am now being locked up in the house while my friends are waiting for me. I am not allowed to play. I am feeling sad and lonely. She doesn't want me to play until I get better. I am missing my friends. I am crying away."

This memory triggered the release of his sadness and physical awkwardness that was stored deep inside his body. He began to feel the tightness in his abdomen. Using body therapy and breathwork, I guided him to express his anguish and demand his mother to nurse his wound. This gradually released the tight feeling from his abdomen.

Next, the visualized scene changed.

"She is now playing hide-and-seek with me and my friends," Rohan described. "We are all laughing. I like my mum this way. She is reminding me about safety and watching me while I play."

The use of the adult intellect to give expression to the inner child had instantly transformed the energy. Rohan now felt his abdomen relaxed and disentangled. Hitherto, the anger in him had made him feel stiff with others and affected his intimacy with his loving wife. Now he saw the correlation between his childhood starvation of warmth and his current awkwardness towards physical affection.

Following this session, Rohan was amazed. He felt grateful because he understood how these early memories had shaped his personality. He had since progressed considerably in his intimacy with his wife, and was also a lot more relaxed during the subsequent therapy sessions.

Regression 2: At Ten Years

At the next session, Rohan asked for the therapy to be focused on his problem of over-complacency and lack of motivation.

After getting him into a hypnotic state, he immediately connected with a memory of himself at the age of ten years. He had stood first in his class performance, and come home with his report card proudly to show his folks. However, what he saw was his parents bickering as usual, over some issues.

"My mother is inside the kitchen and my dad is standing at the kitchen door speaking loudly. There is some tension between them. I am outside in the living room and can see that both of them are angry and not on talking terms. I go in to the kitchen to show my report card, but my father doesn't even notice me. He just storms out of the kitchen as if I don't exist. My mother is in tears."

There was a long pause.

"When I eventually show my report card to my mum, she doesn't look at it. She just dismisses me, saying it's not a good time.

"I am feeling rejected ... so hurt and angry. I am so excited about being first in class. I go into my room crying, feeling so deeply hurt. My teachers and friends are all so happy for me, but my scores have no importance to my parents! I won't bother studying anymore!"

Tears rolled down Rohan's cheeks.

"Why should I bother? Nobody cares!"

Rohan had crystallized the theme of his parents' indifference as being a summary of his childhood experience. He and his brother were silent sufferers of their parents' inattention. He explained how he felt that none of his talents were good enough to grab the attention of his father, who had always been distant. His parents were not on good terms and spent their time in eerie silence. They always focused on their differences and were never happy together. The children had gravitated towards their mother, as their father was physically absent most of the time.

At this point, I guided Rohan's inner child to obtain the support of his parent-self to change things to the way he would have liked it to be.

At the next instance, Rohan visualized his inner child walking into the living room where his father sat reading the newspapers; Rohan called for his mother to drop her kitchen work and come out to join him.

"I want both of you to listen to me. I have come first in my class. Do you hear me? I put in my best and you are not even interested!" He saw his inner child stamping his feet and making fists.

"I want you to see my report card," he said with a thrusting action of both hands.

After a pause he continued, "I now see my parents looking at the report card, feeling happy. My father is now kneeling down to talk to me. He strokes me gently and hugs me. He is appreciating my performance. My mother is absolutely delighted and is talking about throwing a party on my coming birthday."

Rohan's voice sounded more cheerful.

"I see the friends in my group coming to the house. They are celebrating my birthday in a big way. There is a cake, several balloons, caps and lots of colored paper. This is the first time I have had a party. I sense myself so happy cutting the cake. My parents look happy too. My friends and I are gathered together in a circle, playing! My parents are smiling and standing side by side. We all look happy." A sense of relief came over him and tears of joy were rolling down his cheeks.

Rohan concluded this therapy session with a deep sense of satisfaction and a happy facial expression, having finally felt appreciated. He experienced this opportunity to re-parent his inner child with unconditional love and praise. He felt happy, encouraged, and loved. He realized that the simple act of playing the ideal-parent role under trance had been transformational. Following the session, he practiced positive affirmations to both the inner child and adult-self to integrate the above experience.

I saw Rohan again two months after the therapy session. He had made a leap in his progress in terms of warming up to others and feeling physically relaxed. He had also gained some weight and confidence in his work, in which he had started to assert himself and make bold decisions.

Regression 3: At Thirteen Years

For his third session, Rohan was keen to find out what his limiting beliefs were, with regards to money and prosperity, and how that had contributed to his behavioral problems.

Under hypnosis, he connected with an earlier event at the age of thirteen years. Suddenly he experienced pain and vivid body memories.

"My feet are hurting. I am wearing shoes that don't fit me. I have outgrown the size but am still wearing them. My mother says that I should wear them for as long as possible and to school every day," Rohan started to recall.

"I am feeling the hurt badly but proud to wear them as I am able to manage the pain. My mum doesn't want to ask dad for money to buy me new shoes, because it's going to hurt her dignity. She is proud of being able to manage with less money. I am now seeing less of my father, who has always been busy with his work. I am very close to my mother. She is taking care of me and my brother."

Next, Rohan moved to another scene.

"I am carrying a book in my hand to hide a tear in my shorts with it. Mum says she has no money right now to buy new shorts. My brother and I have to make do with what we have. I feel sorry for my mum. I don't want to hurt her. I want to make her happy."

Rohan was surprised to see how he had felt a strong sense of pride in his impoverishment and had tied that to his loyalty to the mother. He realized that he had internalized his mother's egoism as his own feelings and beliefs unconsciously all these years. Living in squalor was his mother's choice, not his. He could now see right through its inappropriateness and wanted to reframe it.

Fig. 1: Rohan's Current Life Regression

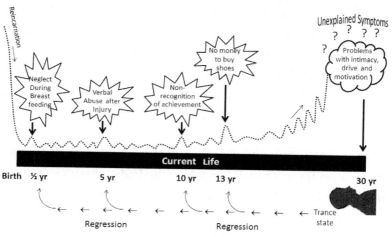

Next Rohan disengaged his identity from the thirteen-year-old child and returned to his adult-self while under trance. Then his adult-self started to engage the child in a dialogue, and explained to the child how he could still have his comforts and yet continue to care for his mother. The adult-self felt the child might have been unfair in not understanding his father over the years.

For the first time, Rohan connected with his inner wisdom and saw how his father had always tried his best to make ends meet. He had been a workaholic all his life. He remained aloof at home and avoided confrontations with his wife. He loved his children and wanted a bright future for them but was unable to express it in words or demonstrate it to them. Rohan was able to empathize with his father and felt that, as a boy, he should have approached his father to cater for his needs, as his mother had failed him.

This was a very fertile moment for him to reconnect with his inner child, during which he re-experienced the feeling of pain in his feet from the ill-fitting shoes.

"What is it that you want to do or see happening that you didn't have the chance the last time?"

"I am now going to my dad. He is busy as usual with his paper work. I am gaining courage to ask for new shoes after telling him what has happened. He chooses to immediately examine the situation and takes me shopping. I am now trying out a pair of new, fitting shoes and I feel so good! My feet don't hurt anymore."

I noted a sense of relief on Rohan's face.

"I am now going to the tailor. We are buying cloth to make my new uniform. The tailor is taking my body measurements, and my father is paying willingly for all this. He asks me if I need anything else. We are buying stationery, books and games. I am so excited! I am shopping for myself, choosing what I want and feeling so good!"

The inner child was delighted. Rohan had untied the distorted belief of "choosing mother equals choosing poverty" and reframed his childhood memory into one of accepting and attracting abundance. He had let go of his coldness towards his father and understood him better. He re-parented his teenage-self by providing unconditional love and integrated it with his adult-self through the visual imagery of shopping with the zest and willingness to spend.

Following the session, Rohan created his reality by putting what he learned into practice. His inner child journey had made a marked difference in his life as he looked at himself with renewed self-esteem and confidence. He was now able to reciprocate the expression of love to others, particularly his doting wife, and to attract abundance in his life. A month later, his life was much brighter as he shopped for new clothes and electronic gadgets for himself. By then he was also looking out to buy a car and a house of his choice!

Conclusion

Inner child healing is only one of the many tools we can use in regression therapy. It makes inroads into the deeper layers of our existence and transcends time to reach the source, to be one again with the infinite treasure of love and bliss that we truly are. The key to it is forgiveness.

"There is a primordial essence characterized by unconditional love, joy, serenity, and wisdom, from which we have become separated and to which we can return by moving out into the vaster realities of awareness."

Ernest Pecci

Through the many transformational journeys of my patients that I have accompanied and their breakthroughs I have witnessed, I have also acquired a new invaluable insight of myself. In particular, inner child therapy has allowed me to connect with my own childhood and conferred me with conscious parenting skills and nurturing principles. My clinical work has enriched me with the wisdom to embrace my unique essence and infuse my inner child with joy, laughter and innocence once again.

Acknowledgment

I owe my personal transformation to my teachers, Dr. Newton Kondaveti and Dr. Lakshmi G.V., who are pioneers of regression therapy in India.

CHAPTER FOUR

Self-Love and Self-Destruction

Dr. Karin Maier-Henle

"It's all very well for me to talk about healing after I've experienced it, or for me to tell you to just trust and let go, letting the flow of life take over, but when you're going through a low period, it's difficult to do – or even know where to begin. However, I think the answer is simpler than it seems, and it's one of the best kept secrets of our time; the importance of self-love."

Anita Moorjani
In: Dying to be Me, 2012

As early as the age of twelve, I have heeded my call to become a physician. After middle school education I continued with night classes and obtained my university entrance qualification. Then I proceeded to study Medicine in Berlin and Munich. In the meantime, I worked part-time as a nurse and a laboratory assistant to save up money for my studies. After graduating from medical school, I continued my training as an internist physician and spent the next eleven years working in hospitals in the specialties of Rheumatology, Gastroenterology and Intensive Care.

I have always enjoyed my clinical training and the medical knowledge gained, but deep within I experienced a desire to be able to practice my medical skills in a more wholesome manner. I began to look beyond Western Medicine to understand the healing process better. Along the way, I acquired my diplomas in Homeopathy, Traditional Chinese Medicine and Acupuncture and expanded my repertoire of healing skills. One day, a paragraph in Hahnemann's *Organon*[9] caught my attention. It stated that any treatment would fail in the long run, if the underlying cause of the problem was still in effect, or if the patient had for various reasons neglected the source, was unaware of the origin, or was in denial of the root of problem. This message was unforgettable as it drastically changed the way I look at therapeutics.

In my career, I had observed a lot of pain in my patients associated with despair and denial while they were struggling with their illnesses. This was particularly pronounced when they were facing death. I found this disconcerting because many of the situations were often also associated with anger, regret, hopelessness, fright and desperation on their part. For the hospital physician, such emotions were generally too tiresome for them to manage. Even if they empathized with their situations, the underlying cause of their angst remained unaddressed. In the search for a method to help me get to the root of my patients' problems, I eventually came across the discipline of regression hypnotherapy.

My Journey as Therapist

Regression is the process of discovering and reliving earlier experiences that have caused the present complaints and condition of the patient. It is a form of transpersonal psychotherapy where forgotten experiences that contain

---

[9] Hahnemann was an 18th-century physician who was dissatisfied with the Medicine of his time and founded Homeopathy. The *Organon* is an overview of his medical system published in 1810.

emotional wounds can be traced back to one's childhood, prenatal period or even to a past life. It is often practiced in association with the use of the hypnotic technique to establish communication with the unconscious mind. The approach uncovers the root of the patient's issues quickly and brings it to the conscious mind. This enables a modification of those unconscious beliefs, actions and behavior that are no longer useful for the patient.

I have grown up in a family background with a pervasive interest in Buddhism. Hence, the concepts of reincarnation and karma were familiar to me from a young age and I have no problems incorporating them into my healing practice. In my journey as a therapist, I have read books by Helen Wambach, Roger Woolger, Andy Tomlinson and Michael Newton. In them, I have found answers to many of my questions as to why certain disorders present in certain individuals the way they do.

As I deepen my knowledge and skills in regression therapy, I keep an open mind to every phenomenon that I encounter. I am aware and convinced that the subconscious mind and soul consciousness can remember feelings and emotions or archive past memories that have resonated with the individual's feelings in some way. I believe a good starting point in any healing practice is to accept and honor stories of such experiences, whenever patients share them. In the early stages of my journey, I have sought help from my Higher Self to resolve the problems of many of my patients who need healing. With time, I have realized that patients need to discover for themselves the meaning of life, and what happens within their inner selves, during illness. They need to come to terms with lessons they are destined to learn in their lifetime. This is because many of the challenges that they face pertain to issues of self-awareness and the mastery of self-love.

Self-Love

Self-love means caring and taking responsibility for one's wellbeing, as well as respecting and knowing oneself. Before one can truly love another person, one needs to love oneself first. Yet I often find self-love is being undervalued and lacking in many people these days.

Many patients, if asked about the existence of self-love, will tend to say, "Yes, of course I love myself." However, as soon as I get to know them better in the process of helping them to manage their problems, it often becomes obvious that the lack of self-love is at the root of their problems. Not uncommonly, their problems are associated with a mix of complex emotional issues including guilt, shame, and blame. When these issues create recurring problems in their lives, emotions like fear, anger or even rage can complicate the picture, and perpetuate a vicious cycle of destructive behavior.

Quite often, the origin of the lack of self-love is not obvious. It is either because it has started too early in life, or is subliminal in nature. Sometimes the trauma of the sensitizing event is so painful that the conscious mind has repressed the memory of the incident.

In my healing practice I find the use of stories helpful. Stories interpret our sensory experiences of life in an unbroken chain of recounted experiences that connect past events to the present as well as to a desired future. They have the capacity to inspire, motivate and highlight the resilience of the human spirit. I believe in telling stories because they function as a powerful stimulus of optimism and hope in distressed patients. In the following section, I share the stories of two of my patients whose lives have remained stuck because of a lack of self-love. After gathering sufficient courage to go through regression therapy, they have since reconnected with their own stories and enhanced the quality of their lives. As they became conscious of the negative experiences they have gone through, they now look forward to more self-loving and life-affirming ways of telling their stories that have since enabled them to heal.

THE CASE OF DANA – LACKING SELF-LOVE

Dana was a dark-haired, fifty-two-year-old lady with a voluptuous beauty. She possessed a sharp wit and a sense of humor, and struck me as a caring individual albeit with a demanding nature. When I first met her, she was at her wits' end, because her younger son had illegally downloaded material from the internet and was facing prosecution. Being a civil servant, she was frightened, deeply embarrassed and unsure of the impact that this situation would have on their lives. We worked through this issue together with a clinical psychologist, and she felt fine for a while. When I met Dana again about two years later, she was coping badly with her aging and ailing mother in addition to a failing relationship. During our conversation, I learned more about her.

Dana was born out of wedlock. Her unruly mother made her pay for the shame involved by openly harassing her and showing hatred. Dana went through some talk therapy together with me and it worked well initially. Shortly afterwards, her mother died of cancer at the age of eighty-two and Dana went into a deep depression. This was quite unlike her, I thought. She had coped very well with many other difficulties in the past, with her rather pragmatic and positive outlook in life. This time, her weight increased rapidly, especially around the tummy area, and that had troubled her immensely.

Dana married young to get away from her mother's influence. Unfortunately, her husband had been disloyal to their marriage relationship. They divorced some years ago, but she still felt a lot of resentment towards him. I also learned about her difficult relationship with her elder son, who refused to have contact with her because her daughter-in-law disliked her. Instead, she loved and found solace in her younger son, who had matured immensely ever since his illegal act two years ago. Interestingly, her younger son was also struggling with an overweight issue.

After her mother's death, Dana had no close relative to rely on and was unsure if she should commit to a new relationship. She admitted she had a problem of low self-worth that was bordering on the verge of self-hate. This was associated with her tendency to indulge in binge eating. Of late, she had felt very lonely and had been experiencing unexplained headaches and a right-knee pain. We could not explain her depression and she agreed to the use of a regression approach to get to the source of her problem.

At the start of the session Dana was positioned comfortably on a reclining couch but she showed signs of nervousness. I suggested that she take a few moments to allow herself to listen to her thoughts and her body.

Hypnotic Induction
When she was ready to relax, I asked her to close her eyes and allow her breathing to become a little slower and deeper. She went well with the experience. Then I facilitated her to establish ideomotor finger-signs, a non-verbal method for the therapist to communicate with the patient's subconscious mind. Next, I conducted a body scan. This was done with my hands positioned several inches over her body with palms facing downwards as intuitive sensors.

"I want you to concentrate on the different areas of your body, as I scan it with my hands for energy that might be stuck in certain locations. That particular part of the body that harbors stuck energy will feel different from its surroundings," I explained as I hovered my palms over various parts of her body. "It can be any part of the body where you feel that something is not right. I will tell you what area I am scanning, as I proceed. You just concentrate on each area and indicate to me if you sense that something is different."

As we went along, I detected tension in her right knee and neck, but the most remarkable finding was in her abdominal region.

"I feel the tension and heaviness in the lower area of my tummy," Dana said. "It is very uncomfortable and feels raw, burning and painful. It feels as if there is something there causing these sensations; something that doesn't really belong to me, but is giving me the pain."

This put me on the alert. What Dana described had just affirmed the feeling of stuck energy I had detected with my palms.

Thought Form

The concept of "stuck" energy or emotion is akin to an individual trying to hum a tune but finding that he just cannot seem to get the tune out of his head. Very often, such stuck emotion is due to a negative memory association. I needed to delineate its origin, and so I encouraged Dana to voice the thoughts that were forming in her mind.

"I want you to concentrate on this energy in your tummy, and as you do so, I am moving it to your voice box … and we will hear from you what the origin of this energy is."

The result was astonishing and startling.

115

"This is my mother's energy," Dana said. Shortly afterwards, she felt agitated with it.

"I can feel it. It feels just like her ... she is there, with me." She described the energy with emotion.

In regression therapy, such a concentration of a person's thought energy is occasionally encountered and recognized as a "thought form". In theosophical discourse, each definite thought produces a radiating vibration. The radiating vibration appears in both the mental and astral bodies of the individual. When this is being sent out from either the mental or astral body, it immediately clothes itself in the elemental essence that vivifies the matter of the mental and astral planes. The thought then becomes a kind of "living creature", the thought-force being the soul, and the vivified matter being the body.

This thought form can also attach to another individual and behaves like a sub-personality. In Dana's case, the materialized thought from the mother had taken on a physical form and attached to her as tension in her abdomen.

The concept of thought form is mentioned in Tibetan Buddhism. There are two schools of thought with regards to its origin. In the "one-life-only" school of thought, it could be conceived that the deep negative bond shared between Dana and her mother had imprinted on her subconscious mind. This created a negative field inside her as she coped to resolve her internal conflicts, following her mother's death. In the school embraced the extended perspective of past life existence, the detected energy is just like what Dana felt it was – her mother's energy. The mother's soul consciousness that left the body after death had attached itself to Dana's energy field, and contributed to her negative emotions.

Regardless of the explanation, Dana needed to get rid of the negative energy that had caused her depression. After all, this could be achieved quickly while in the hypnotic state and all that was needed was Dana's own mental resources. I next communicated directly with this energy in the same way as I would have done with a sub-personality of the patient.

"Hi, I am Karin and am here to help. I would like to speak to the energy that is here within Dana. Is it true that you are Dana's mother?"

"Yes, it's true," the energy spoke, and it was through Dana's voice box, "I am indeed Dana's mother."

"Can you let us know why you are here?" I asked.

"After that miserable life that I lived, I have decided to stay here with Dana as I want her to pay for some of the negative experiences I have endured in my life."

"But what makes you feel you need to do that?"

"I don't want to be alone in this misery. I want her to be as miserable as I am, and I will not leave her before I have accomplished this."

"I see." I paused as I was mentally structuring my response. "I believe you may not be aware of the fact that you do have other far more promising and satisfying choices, where you neither need to remain in misery nor stay in the body. Perhaps you may want to consider these other options?"

It was a gradual, persuasive process. I gently coaxed the mother's energy to leave Dana's body as the preferred option. We exchanged views and arguments during our dialogue while Dana remained in trance. The energy was initially quite persistent about remaining in the body, being very bitter and determined, but I managed to convince her to leave.

Interestingly, after the mother's energy agreed to leave, she played a trick on us!

After I presumed the energy had left after my persuasion, I did a check scan of Dana's body. When I came to the abdominal area again, Dana cried out: "She has left her belly with me! She has left it right here!"

This was a surprise! I had to re-persuade the residual energy again to leave. Eventually all traces of the energy left to return to the Light. This included all imprints, hooks or seeds, and there was no foothold to allow for a return. I next implemented an energy protection for Dana before proceeding with the therapy proper.

Age Regression

I deepened Dana's trance state, and Dana regressed back to the time when she was eight years old.

It was a frightening event and a horrifying experience. Her mother had gone out of the house and left her alone in the flat, locking her in.

"I am terrified. I feel devastated," Dana said. "She has trapped me in the house. I am so frightened that I have to escape from the house through a window. Later, a neighbor finds me and takes care of me until my mother returns," she sobbed.

"My mother subsequently sends me to a boarding school. Over there, I feel better and safer. I am able to make friends."

As the childhood story unfolded under trance, there were other similarly unpleasant situations that were retrieved. Her mother had abused her and called her names and had behaved irresponsibly as a parent.

At the next significant event, she regressed back to the time when she was three years of age. There were very sad memories.

"My mum is leaving me with my grandmother," she recalled. "Her mind is all made up and she does not care one bit for me."

"What are your feelings now?" I asked.

"Lonely and abandoned. The feeling is that of shock and unfamiliarity," she said. The trauma of being deserted had weighed heavily on her emotions.

Next, I regressed Dana back to the time she was in her mother's womb.

The therapeutic rationale behind a prenatal regression is based on the understanding that our most basic emotional programming begins before birth. At this stage, the growing fetus is perceived as a sentient being that absorbs and responds to information from its mother and the uterine environment. At the same time, its expectations of life are being formulated according to the mother's mental state.

Once within the womb, Dana visualized her fetal body contours, her umbilical cord attachment to the mother and the surrounding amniotic fluid environment. Most of all, she could sense her mother's heartbeat and emotions distinctly. She remarked, "I feel my mother's loneliness. I feel her anger too. She is in a rage at being pregnant under such circumstances. I am afraid this isn't going to be easy for both of us ... I am frightened."

Spirit Realm

From the womb I next directed her to the spirit realm to meet her guide. Of interest, once in this realm, she discovered that she had set herself up for some challenging lessons as part of her Life Plan.

"I am talking to my spirit guide, whom I know is wise and fair. I can feel his love for me and I am at peace. He congratulates me on being so brave and making such profound progress. He tells me that I should work on self-love. I realize that I have chosen my current body, because I want to have an additional challenge of being heavy and having to work hard to find balance. It is nice though, to be strong and resilient, and I feel I have made the right choice. I am very ambitious and working on tolerance and acceptance. I also want to experience being independent."

Fig. 2: Dana's Single-session Therapy

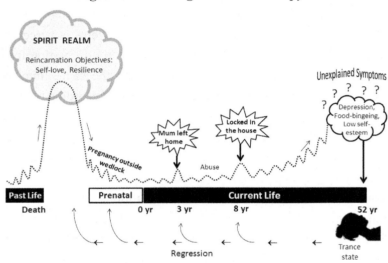

Next Dana met her mother in the spirit realm. To her surprise, their roles were reversed in a past life! With this new insight and the understanding of the implications involved, she felt that she could now let go.

"I see that I have been cruel to her in that past life when I've abused and abandoned her. I can feel how she suffered then. We have decided that we would reverse our roles in this life, so that we both have the opportunity to experience the neglect, helplessness and anger of an abused child. We plan to experience the emotion of having to overcome what we have to endure. I know I want to let go, and it is important for us to find self-love and forgiveness while we are still incarnated. It is not always possible to attain all our goals in a lifetime, but we have many chances to learn what we desire to. It is a lot more difficult when we are experiencing all the negative feelings while being in the body. I am aware now of our plans for this current life and I am alright with it."

Both Dana and her mum could let go of what had happened after they found love for each other. She discovered that she was a very ambitious soul who had chosen to journey through a very demanding life, which could turn out well if she succeeded in learning how to forgive and overcome her prejudice.

Inner Child Healing

After the meeting with her mother, I felt Dana needed more profound healing at this stage.

I next facilitated Dana to meet her eight-year-old self in the spirit realm. The adult and young Dana connected with each other wonderfully. At my suggestion, they blew up colored balloons together side by side, with different colors that represented different meanings.

They chose a green balloon for being healthy, accepting and caring for that body; a red one for eating healthily and knowing what is good for herself; a white one for tolerance; a yellow one for the ability to say no if she meant it; a pink one for self-love, independence and joy for things she encountered in this life; a brown one for being able to see things from different perspectives; an orange one for joy in moving her body and doing sports; and a multi-colored one with all the abilities she might need but could not come up with now.

The use of the balloon metaphor to strengthen little Dana's inner support structure was fundamental in enhancing her ability to work through her deep-seated and blocked emotions. As a child who had been neglected and abused, Dana had grown up too fast and skipped too many important experiences vital for a healthy development. The inflating of different balloons representing different attributes that she had missed would enhance the child's sense of self, and this was crucial towards healthy emotional expression. Getting young Dana to blow up balloons involved the act of deep breathing, loosening up, knowing her body and feeling the power within it. In this inner child work, the blowing of balloons that carried different meanings involved tapping into the child's own individuality and experiences where the expressions were metaphorical representations of her life. The act was symbolic of creating self-attributes. This encouraged her to know and empower herself. By focusing on the self, Dana was integrating the affirmation "This is who I am" into her awareness.

Next, the adult and little Dana admired each other lovingly. "I can see little Dana being so happy now; she is beautiful and her eyes shine so brightly." Adult Dana kept the little Dana in her arms and looked at her with a concentrated focus. Then I guided her to visualize little Dana shrinking gradually in size, eventually to about the size of an orange. At this point, adult Dana put the orange-sized Dana into her heart to be united with herself as one, as it was always meant to be.

It was a wonderful healing experience!

With the insight and wisdom gained from revisiting her past, Dana could anchor herself on her strengths now, and became more aware that she had all the necessary power and assistance to work on her life lessons.

Dana felt significantly energized after the session. She turned bubbly and could not wait to change some of the things that needed to change. She had a feeling that something within her was significantly different after her mother's death but had not wanted to pay too much attention to it until now.

Follow-up

I reviewed Dana some weeks later. It was wonderful to find her happy and significantly improved in her mood. What surprised me was that Dana was physically much fitter than before. Her case was unique. A single therapy session had produced a significant and swift transformation.

"I feel so much better now. The depression is gone completely," she reported. "I realize that there are still a lot of things I want to change, and I know now I can do it. I have enrolled in a fitness studio, and the strange thing is I really like it! I thought I may faint the first time I step on a treadmill, but now I am fine even after exercising on it for as long as twenty-five minutes. I feel great after the workout. I have lost eight pounds since and I am not going to stop anytime soon. I feel strong and confident and have made plans for a lot of other things that I want to experience."

Dana then shared her thoughts on her self-awareness.

"I no longer feel like I am a victim even if something does not work out as planned. It has a lot to do with what is happening to me, and I can see where I can change things, or adapt to new situations a lot more easily. The therapy session that we had was so helpful. I can now deal with all the painful memories of the difficult times I had with my mother."

THE CASE OF LAURA – SELF-DESTRUCTIVE PATTERNS

The second patient, Laura, was someone close to my heart, because I had known her for a long time. As a warm, caring person with a deep connection with her surroundings, she was surprisingly unaware of her loving nature and her potential. Like Dana, she too had a very low self-esteem and always felt that she was to be blamed if something went wrong. She had an unexplained fear that bad things might happen to her, even though there wasn't any basis for that. Furthermore, she had been bothered by a feeling that she had always been letting other people down.

As a child, Laura was emotionally unwanted by her mother and she had to confront her parents' marriage problems very early on in her life. This probably contributed to her deep-seated feelings of unworthiness. She was forty-seven years old when she was ready to accept my offer of hypnotherapy for her treatment. By then, she had been married for twenty-five years to a man much older than her. Despite her strong, motherly nature, she had consciously chosen not to have children.

Laura felt very guilty that she had not committed herself to motherhood. Previous attempts with different approaches to amend her negative feelings and improve her self-image had met with only short-term success. This time we agreed to explore her problem with the use of regression therapy.

Difficult Induction

Laura went through a hypnotic induction with deep relaxation exercises, but unfortunately had difficulty getting into a hypnotic state. Communication through her ideomotor finger signals revealed that her subconscious mind was afraid to let go and lose control. I then used a different approach.

I guided her to imagine herself watching a movie on a cinema screen and anticipate the next coming scene. I got her to see that as an analogy to hypnosis and an aid to enter the trance state. Unfortunately this approach also failed. Then I figured out that she needed a safe environment. To strengthen her sense of security, I asked her to seek additional help by choosing a power animal. This would strengthen her inner self and fortify her own energy field.

The concept of the power animal and its application in regression therapy is explained in the previous chapter. It turned out that Laura lacked the courage to even make the move all by herself. I had to go one step further. I guided her to the spirit realm and summoned her spirit guide to assist her in the choice of the power animal.

Amazingly, Laura returned from the spirit realm with a yellow duck and grinned. To my knowledge, the duck represented a multitalented animal that could walk, swim and fly, and therefore symbolized flexibility to blend into various situations. The yellow color reminded me of the popular, squeezable duck toy that we normally associate with children during bath time. To my mind, the animal would therefore assume the function of a symbol for lively infants and children. When I asked Laura about her choice, she explained that her duck was a symbol that she should lighten up during the therapy session, and that nothing untoward would happen. It was an amusing explanation, and the power animal worked well.

Regression 1: Past Life – Man and Cowardice

Soon Laura attained a sufficient depth of trance, and started to sense feelings from some of the past life characters on the movie screen that I suggested earlier. I understood that to be a sign that she was ready for regression.

Laura was brought back to a past life in the nineteenth century as a lonely, wandering man who earned a living through woodwork and carpentry. He led a simple and solitary life, but found himself in a scary situation. He had the terrible task of facing and handling a group of robbers who were seated around a campfire in a wood. These robbers were heartless; they plundered and killed. He was very frightened and wanted to hide from them. On the one hand, he couldn't compromise on his moral principles to commit crimes with them, and on the other hand he was afraid that they would kill him if they knew his reluctance. In the end, he decided that he had to run away or risk losing his life. Under the pretense of cooperating with them, he found an opportunity to escape.

"What happened after you got away?" I asked.

"I am on the run. I never got to slow down. I am looking out for them. I end up wandering to various places to look for jobs while on the alert, to avoid being discovered."

"How do you look like in this past life?"

"I am feisty and not too big in size."

"Which country are you in?"

"The landscape reminds me of either the Netherlands or Belgium, during the era around 1800 to 1850."

"What are your feelings as a man in this life?"

"I feel like I am walking down a dark road … but unafraid. I am doing woodwork for a living. I know it is hard work and I don't really mind."

"What thoughts are associated with these feelings?"

"In this life, I am always solitary and cautious. I listen carefully and talk very little. I am quite contented with what I do for a living. I have never had a place that belongs to me, nor felt that I belong anywhere. I have accepted that this is how it has to be, for someone in my situation."

It was clear that he did not bemoan his fate, and had accepted his life as it was. I next directed him to the end of that life. At the death-bed, he saw himself as a tired, elderly man who was worn out. He was almost completely bald and had lots of wrinkles. He was lying in a bed within a small room in someone else's house and feeling exhausted.

"What are the thoughts on your mind just before your heart stopped beating?"

"I feel as if my light went out ... just like the candle I see in that room. All my vital energy is consumed. There is nothing left in me. I have no hard feelings, and there is no need for me to hang on ..."

The death process was uneventful. He hovered over the dying body for a while, after which the soul energy left readily. On entering the spirit realm, I encouraged him to meet other souls of that lifetime. Some interesting insights emerged.

He first met the souls of the robbers. They revealed that it was his choice to live a wandering life. His life lesson was in fact to experience cowardice! Next, he met the victims of the robbers. He was told that it was his choice not to make any soul contract with the victims and that he had no obligation to interfere with their outcomes. The primary lesson was for him to experience what it meant, and felt like, to be a coward in that life.

As we were integrating all these experiences, two of Laura's character traits in her current life were brought to her attention. Firstly, she was reminded of her strong aversion to other people who showed the slightest hint of being a coward. Through this past life experience, it transpired on a higher level of consciousness, that this natural reaction of hers had a basis. Secondly, she firmly believed that in her current life she was not able to succeed on her own. In contrast, in that past life her male-self did survive independently, and well enough. He was an excellent listener and judge of things that he had quietly overheard each time he entered a new city or village to look for a job. He was able to blend in socially with other people without interfering with their lives. He was self-sufficient and able to leave other people alone, which was something Laura had trouble with in her current life.

Furthermore, Laura in her current life had always struggled with loneliness and the sense of non-belonging. She now understood that all these were the result of carried-over energies from the previous life.

"I can see now that these feelings of being unworthy and a coward who lets people down and sacrifices himself do not belong to me in my current life," Laura said. "My guide tells me that I have to learn to love myself, appreciate things for what they are and enjoy life while discovering what it means to be happy and relaxed."

We ended the session with a grounding exercise as described by Helen Wambach. It was a visualization script that described a tightly budded rose growing from the solar plexus and receiving white light and healing energy from a sacred place as it slowly opened its petals in the process. In a wonderful manner, Laura described her rose as a briar rose, with a beautiful yellow center as the receptacle for the energy.

Regression 2: Past Life – Man with Bliss

A week later, Laura wrote to me to say that she had found a sense of calmness and confidence even though her day-to-day life remained rough. She felt relieved, because she had succeeded in disconnecting herself from the feelings of cowardice, non-belonging and loneliness.

A few more weeks passed before Laura came for her second healing session. This time, she regressed back to a beautiful life in which she visualized herself as a middle-aged man who was calm, centered and wholesome. He was a member of a group of natives who lived in a rain-forest and was well adapted to his natural environment. A scene of him rowing a canoe on a river emerged. Following the scene of the river trip, she caught a view of a beautiful lake with a waterfall in the background. Next was another serene scene where he was sitting around a fire with other members of his tribe, feeling very connected, peaceful and calm with a strong sense of belonging.

It was a life of love and perfection with experiences of peace and belonging. There were no crises in the story, no shutdowns and no catharsis during the regression. The life was devoid of fear, anger, worries and stress.

The death-point in this life was again related to the theme of water. He was swimming with river dolphins and experienced an intuitive feeling that his time had come. At that point, he calmly surrendered himself to the end of his life. There were no bad feelings; only tranquility and peace prevailed. It had been a perfectly beautiful life, in which he was able to experience a strong and capable body and enjoy social equality with his group members. He felt himself as being part of nature, wholesome and fulfilled. All he did seemed effortless and he was very thankful for a life that was in perfect order.

After his energies left his body, he saw himself going to a beautiful place where there was a big meadow with a round niche and a round stone bank built in, overlooking a green, beautiful valley below. He sat there in peace. Next to him was his spirit guide, who was also looking down on the valley and said, "See, I told you it was easy, wasn't it?" At that point, they both chuckled as they looked down the valley together. He found himself tearing up because it was so beautiful and so full of love to be home.

When Laura was integrating the experience of this session, she thought the lesson from this past life was to experience living in a body without physical aches and pains or social pressures.

'It was an effortless life that was free from fear or anger. I appreciate that very much because it has given me peace and tranquility. Now I know that there is still a part of me that is able to be still, peaceful and wholesome."

It was a different style of existence and a contrast to what Laura had been experiencing in her current life. She loved the experience of pureness and unconditional love and responded positively to the therapy session. She felt as if a light deep inside her had been turned on, and everything was in its rightful place and interconnected.

When Laura and I met up again after some time, she was going through a stressful period and needed urgent help.

Regression 3: Past Life – Woman and Wartime
Laura's husband had fallen ill with lymphoma and needed chemotherapy and radiation treatment. Her parents had been giving her a hard time. She needed more time with her husband and could no longer attend to her parents as often as before. She felt sad as her work performance had dropped. At the same time, she felt very tense and tired and had trouble with her sleep. She was aware that she was holding on to a lot of fear and anger.

In the course of our conversation, I realized what she wanted out of the therapy session this time was to understand why she had always felt fearful and insecure about losing her loved ones.

After relaxing her on the couch, Laura regressed back to a past life as a woman peasant during the period of the Thirty Years' War (1618–48) in Europe. It was a war motivated by religious conflicts within the Holy Roman Empire and consisted of a series of wars fought mainly in Central Europe. Being long drawn, there was devastation of entire regions denuded by the foraging armies and made worse by famine and disease. As the years passed, the whole community where Laura and her husband were staying lost nearly everything. They were robbed several times by hordes of soldiers who took away all their food and possessions.

She entered that past life at the point of a particularly difficult winter when nearly everyone had left the village, because it was almost completely destroyed. Many children and elderly people were abandoned and left behind while she and her husband stayed back to take care of them. They were left alone in the settlement, fighting desperately to survive. Many people fell ill and some perished from poverty and hunger. They never really got to a point where they had sufficient food or felt secure enough for a decent existence. Laura was very bitter because people who had been dear to her had left. She became withdrawn and diffident, and never felt safe.

At the death point, she saw herself as an old, frail woman with gray hair. She felt lonely. She had been tending to their only remaining cow in the stable, and she described how close her feelings were to that animal. Feeling very tired, she leaned against the cow for support. Then she sat down, curled herself up and died without pain or struggle. Her last thought was that it had been a hard life, and that she was abandoning those who were still with her and needed her help, including her husband. As her energies were leaving the body, she noted her old wrinkled body that was thin and worn out.

In the spirit realm, she met her spirit guide and found herself again in a beautiful meadow. This time there was a big, sturdy apple tree that provided a comfortable shade. She noticed that the meadow was fenced in with a rustic fence, and her spirit guide smilingly joked about the feature as being representative of her need to feel secure!

Laura and her guide talked about the meaningful way she had lived that past life, as a result of the care and love she had given to the young and old people left behind in the village during the war. She had been resilient and sincere, and had worked hard to help others to survive. However, she had also become bitter because so many people, whom she held dear to her heart, had abandoned her. Only in the spirit realm did she understand that those who left her had to leave to survive, and give the rest who stayed behind a chance to survive too. She realized that this was a lesson she had opted to learn in that life, and again in her current life.

Next, she met the soldiers who had robbed the village. Again, that was part of their Life Plan. She had no bad feelings for them after learning that. She met her past life husband in the spirit realm and he turned out to be the same husband in her current life. They had arranged to work through their issues that were left over from the past life together. These were issues of trust and confidence.

Recollecting her lonely, fugitive experiences in her first past life regression, she suddenly developed a new insight. She now appreciated the feelings and thinking of those people who likewise ran away from her village in this past life. She appreciated that they had no other option but to leave, or else all of them would starve to death together. It was a huge relief now that she was able to see things from this perspective. This new insight helped her to overcome her grudge towards them. It was the forgiveness she was able to grant them that she felt was really important. The lesson she had distilled from that lifetime was to learn to let go, trust people, forgive and to savor whatever she had in life.

"One of the things most helpful to me was that I realized I still have a lot of options. Staying back to help others was my choice," Laura said when she was integrating her experience.

"I am also very grateful to learn that, in addition to the people I have now in my life, I will be meeting other souls in the future. They will be helping me, and together we will accomplish the goals we have set for ourselves."

With this new insight Laura felt she was now more prepared and confident to anticipate and face the loss of her loved ones.

Regression 4: Current Life Regression

When Laura and I next met, she expressed her wish to explore the origin of her deep-seated feelings of low self-esteem and worthlessness. These issues had been puzzling her for a long time. After some discussion, we decided that we would make contact with her inner child.

Upon induction, Laura went quickly to an early childhood event that was at the root of her feeling of worthlessness. She was about six years old then. She saw her mother dressed up with her coat on, sitting on the bed in her bedroom looking withdrawn and distant. She and her sister were begging her not to desert them. Laura said she could feel her mum's unhappiness as if it was something that she could touch. Her mum's face was hard and cold. She said to them, "It's because of you two that I had to give up my life opportunities. You are the reason that I am unhappy. I cannot and do not want to stay. I am leaving."

At that point, Laura said she felt as if the ground beneath her feet was swaying and giving way. She also experienced numbness and difficulty in breathing. These were sensations that she had not experienced before.

Fig. 3: Laura's Current Life Regression

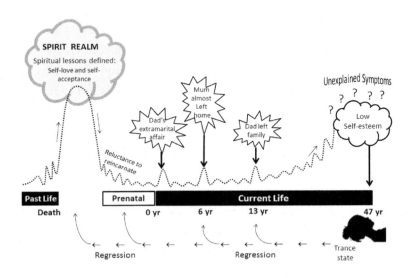

She and her sister continued to beg their mother to stay. She felt as if her stomach was wrenching and the whole world was crashing down, piece by piece, around her. Eventually her mother gave in, but very reluctantly. The two girls were made to go back into their room where they held and comforted each other in misery.

At the next significant event, Laura was twelve years old and encountered an unpleasant situation. She was going through puberty, and very conscious of her physical appearance. She had been belittled by some of her schoolmates who shamed her. In sadness, she turned to her mother for solace. To her disappointment and horror, all her mother said was, "Do not blame me for your ugliness. That is not my fault!"

Laura couldn't understand her mother's response. It was as if her brain was short-circuited and needed to be re-booted. She pressed the heels of her hands into her eyes and saw nothing but sparkles!

The next unforgettable incident occurred during a family holiday when she was thirteen years old. Her father had suddenly changed his plans to leave the children alone at home with their mother and went on the trip alone. While seeing him off, her mother got into a rage because she felt badly deserted.

Subsequently, the story came to light that their father had an affair with another woman, shortly after Laura was born. Her mother had put the blame on the children because she had to stay home to take care of them and could not accompany the father. Since the affair, her parents had lived apart for nearly a year. Her mother had moved to her uncle's home with the children, while leaving their father alone to decide on what he wanted of the marriage. The negative emotion associated with the event was later described by Laura as being similar to an intensified version of the helplessness and hopelessness that she experienced at the age of six, when her mother almost deserted her.

To complete the regression experience, I brought Laura back to her mother's womb. While in the womb, she was receiving several impressions that her postnatal life was not going to be easy. It occurred to her that the purpose of her current life was to find the truth, and stand up to her situational challenges, especially those coming from her parents' disharmony. She had to work on the emotional issues of abandonment, self-love, self-worth, independence and guilt. She also sensed that she had been very reluctant to incarnate into this life, but knew it was an opportunity to learn and grow.

She was next directed to the spirit realm where she could talk to the souls involved in her spiritual journey. She tuned into one of the meetings where the current life was discussed, and the event was played out on a stage with a theatre-like quality to it. All the main "players" were there and were discussing the lesson she was supposed to learn in her current life. Apparently the lessons for her, her parents, her sister and her husband were intertwined. Her parents had chosen to experience a life where they had to tolerate anger, illness and a lack of love.

Next she visualized the imagery of herself standing at a crossroads in a huge room with several tubular openings and passageways, each leading to a different future incarnation. She was involved in a serious discussion with the souls of her current sister and husband with regards to the choice of physical body to reincarnate into. Next, she watched them each embarking on their own reincarnation journey, and felt somewhat desperate as they were departing. Finally, she turned to her spirit guide, who encouraged her to take her own leap. She then visualized herself stepping into one of the tubular openings. The door closed and the passageway collapsed behind her. The feeling was heavy, and she knew she was committed to a journey of no return.

Laura said to me that her entire soul group[10] had worked together on some of her life problems before. She had chosen to reincarnate in a weak body and could not afford to be distracted from the learning of her lessons this time. She wanted to work on the issues of self-love, self-acceptance and the feeling of helplessness and abandonment, because these were her areas of weaknesses.

---

[10] A soul group is a group of soul beings who help the individual to learn life lessons. Many of them have made agreements with the individual to meet at some juncture in their Earth-bound lives, have been with him in previous incarnations and spent the majority of their time with him in those lives.

While still in the spirit realm, I took the opportunity to conduct inner child healing for her. She retreated to a favorite place where her adult self could meet up with the thirteen-year-old Laura. They had a long and wonderful talk about self-acceptance and her sense of loyalty, which was her current life strength. They developed additional qualities that they would like to strengthen together. This included the ability to say no, to stay powerful, be independent, trust one's own intuition, appreciate life, love oneself and to forgive. Since both little and adult Laura loved ice cream, I suggested that they could represent these qualities by different categories of Italian ice cream, each with a different color and flavor for each quality they wanted to represent. They shared the ice cream cones together, and then reaffirmed their love for each other. They also affirmed the correctness of their decision to reincarnate into the current life. Finally, I guided them to visualize the gradual union of their separate energies into one whole and single being of light.

When Laura came out of trance, she felt not only a sense of calm, but also of melancholy from revisiting all the pertinent childhood events. Deep in thought, she indicated that she needed time to digest and integrate all the regression experience into her current situation.

Laura returned for a follow-up a few days later. She had significantly improved and reported that she was able to relax and sleep better after the last session. In addition she was also able to resist her temptation for sweet things.

Regression 5: Past Life as African Boy

In the next session, Laura requested to work on her body aches and pains, as she believed that those symptoms came from a non-physical origin. After some thought, I decided to use a somatic bridge by directing her to focus on her back muscles where her discomfort was most disturbing. By now, she was quite accustomed to the regression process and she could enter a trance state seamlessly. As she focused on her back pain, a thought readily emerged.

"I am not good, I let everybody down," she said. As I got her to focus her concentration on that thought further, she connected readily with a past life.

She saw herself as an eight-year-old, black-skinned boy with curly hair, and was swimming in an ocean. He belonged to an African tribe. He was supposed to look after the goats that were enclosed behind a stone wall. Unfortunately he had forgotten to close the gates securely before he left. The goats escaped, were hunted down by wild animals and many were killed. He was desperate and could not believe that this had happened, but he admitted his mistake of overlooking the secureness of the gate. The tribe decided to cast him out of the community as a warning for all the other boys in the tribe. A sympathetic old man within the community pleaded for him, but to no avail. He had to leave.

After wandering around as a fugitive, the boy settled down in a shallow ditch and surrendered himself to fate. He was exhausted and gave up looking for food. He felt deeply shameful and was devastated. He mentally revisited situations where the old man had reminded him to be more cautious, but being very lively and easily distractible, he had to learn things the hard way. Eventually he died from starvation with soreness all over his body.

At the death point, his last thought was "I have let everybody down. I am no good."

As his heart stopped beating, he said to himself: "All this went terribly wrong! I made the same mistake again. I did not pay attention and make good use of my opportunity."

After his energies left the body he went to the spirit realm to meet his spirit guide, who appeared in a lovely, female form. The guide helped him to understand that the main theme of the life lesson was about responsibility and overcoming his "Johnny-head-in-the-air" attitude.

In her current life, Laura was a very sweet soul and loved to help, but did not like the burden of taking on responsibility for other people. This past life experience helped her to understand that she needed to put her feelings of obligations to her parents in context. Her parents had chosen a life without love, or the ability to love each other as spouses. She was now clear that, as their offspring, she was not the source of their unhappiness. She had done her duty as daughter. Her parents, on their part, had chosen to learn their lesson on marital conflict in the current life. Regardless of her presence, her parents would not have been happy, unless and until they were able to love each other. It was not her obligation to find solutions for them.

The boy met with the souls of the other tribesmen who decided to cast him out. He learned that they had not meant to be cruel, but had to uphold their rules of behavior for everyone in the tribe to survive. They, too, had suffered the consequences of the loss of the goats. They apologized but believed that they had made that decision in the bigger interest of the entire tribe. They all had important lessons to learn and these included coping with grief, loyalty, trust and safety.

Through this therapy session, Laura discovered that the body pain was carried over from the past life. After reframing the event, she could integrate important lessons and address the issues of being reckless, carefree and irresponsible. She had worked extensively on these issues in other lives, and it seemed that this repetitive pattern could be finally resolved through striking a delicate balance in her current life.

We ended the session with some future pacing and it worked out well. She saw herself as a responsible, kind and thoughtful woman who would not take blame when it was not appropriate. She was forgiving to herself and others if things did not work out well and she would just stay focused on working out the right balance. She felt very good with the experience.

A fortnight later Laura wrote to me:

"Dear Doctor,

It's been 14 days since our last session. The changes that I am going through are positive and astounding at times. I have found that as the days passed, my automatic self-deprecation has waned and I am able to accept and enjoy the feeling that I am a loved and valued spark of the limitless and undying love, as we all are. So far I have not, except for a few difficult occasions, felt it necessary to put a damper on this magnificent and liberating feeling. During these few occasions, I was able to snap out of negativity after a short while. As you can see, things look very promising. The interaction with my parents has become easier, as I do not feel as guilty as I did before. I realize now that this guilt has been felt by them and irritated them. Keeping fingers crossed, we seem to be able to relax in each other's presence. Thank you for going through this journey with me."

Since then, I have heard from Laura a few more times. She struck me as someone who had awakened and gone through a powerful transformation.

Concluding Thoughts

Dana and Laura were exemplars of patients who had suffered abuse or neglect in their early childhood and presented in their later life with a lack of self-love or self-destructive behavior.

Often, such patients had parents who didn't love them. Sometimes, they grew up without parents or anyone who could give them a home or sense of belonging. Many of them were abandoned and grew up in loneliness and lacking happiness or affection. They often blamed themselves for what they were because they were conditioned to believe that they deserved to be blamed. Yet, the real problem stemmed from the unreliability and volatile behavior of the very people they were dependent on. Sometimes they might even have been physically abused.

Many such patients lacked a platform for natural confidence that normal children grew up with. It could take a very long time to work on compensating this loss to become the person they wanted to be. In the absence of a foundation for self-love and self-acceptance, it could be very difficult to quit unhealthy habits. Occasionally, various types of addictive behavior could result. It could take a lot of courage to face the challenge of enduring emotional hardships early in life; the agony might eat into their health until such time they started to look for help. One way or other, they needed to overcome their frustration, self-hatred and self-destructive behavior. Some of them had treated themselves badly for years or even decades. They felt small, gave in to others and even subconsciously honored the way they were ill-treated by significant others. Some of them became negative and embraced the same kind of abusive behavior and disrespect for others. It would take courage to start looking for the source of their problem and make significant changes in their lives.

There are many different ways to initiate change. Some patients made it on their own while others received help from counseling or psychotherapy. Regression therapy is one option and it has the advantage of being able to help the individual to connect to the source of the problem. Sometimes one needs to go beyond the current life to look for karmic connections and lessons to be learned from a past life. While it is challenging to go to the core of one's issues, the outcome can be a very rewarding and transformational experience.

Certain prerequisites are necessary. The individual must accept hypnosis, trust the therapist and have good rapport with him. It takes patience, repetition and sometimes practice before one can enter into a trance state. He must stop perceiving himself as a helpless victim and be prepared to unravel the truth behind his suffering.

Once healing sets in, the patient is more able to balance his views, and appreciate the good things of life. He may like to change things that are changeable and make peace with things that are not within his influence. He may also find it easier to let go. When he has understood the origin of his issues and appreciates the complex interrelationships between people in his life, he will be able to change the way he thinks about what happens to him in his life. The enlightenment can be liberating to a degree beyond his expectations.

A colleague of mine, Herve Mignot, who works in Palliative Care in France, once told me, "We should never, as long as we are alive, limit ourselves or others to the current state or belief-system we are in at the moment. We can always rise above it if we want to, and when we are ready."

CHAPTER FIVE

Struggling for Love

Dr. Sérgio Werner Baumel

"Even though no one can go back and make a new beginning, anyone can start now and make a new ending."
Francisco Cândido Xavier

I went into regression therapy through an unusual route. At an earlier stage of my life, I had wanted to be a researcher because I was interested in investigating the function of the brain. However, I was advised to first study Medicine as a stepping stone towards achieving that goal. I took the advice, but upon graduating from medical school, I changed my mind and specialized in Clinical Neurology instead.

Several years later, while practicing as a neurologist, I observed that many of my patients had psychological rather than neurological problems. Added to this was the pleasant surprise that many of them had also asked me if I could be their therapist. I understood this to be because they liked the way I talked to them.

While I was toying with the idea of taking up psychotherapy, I came to learn about the principle of reincarnation through my contact and interaction with some spiritual groups. The idea seemed plausible to me although I remained skeptical for a while. Eventually, when I read Dr. Brian Weiss' first books on past life therapy, *Many Lives, Many Masters* and *Only Love Is Real,* my perspective changed. Dr. Weiss was a renowned physician whom I respected. He had never heard about Spiritism[11] nor any Afro-Brazilian religions[12] and yet he produced clinical evidence that matched the reincarnation principle as taught in these religions.

My Journey as Therapist

My initial experience with regression techniques was a positive one. I was pleasantly surprised at the ease with which people could be brought into a hypnotic state, and thereafter guided into a past life experience. I was equally surprised with the good therapeutic outcome obtainable with this approach. Soon, I took up studies in psychology and hypnosis, and went on to develop my skills in regression therapy.

Regression therapy turned out to be a very effective and efficient form of therapy in my experience. I continued to obtain good results in my patients with a variety of clinical problems. Soon, I discerned a pattern. In my psychotherapy practice, people usually come asking for help with symptoms such as headaches, anxiety, panic attacks, insomnia, depression, etc. They rarely related those symptoms to their relationships or their feelings of not being loved. Yet, when I used the regression approach to delineate the root of their symptoms, relationship issues often surfaced as the primary problem.

Of interest, I had observed that a significant number of my patients who were married women claimed that their husbands were good men and that they were happily married. However,

---

[11] Spiritism is a spiritual doctrine codified by Allan Kardec in 1859. It embraces the concept of reincarnation as a way of perfecting one's moral self until it fits into God's presence.

[12] Afro-Brazilian religions are syncretic religions. Brazil has a rich spiritual society formed from the confluence of the Catholic Church with the religious traditions of the indigenous African people.

under regression therapy they changed those statements. They admitted that they had been fooling themselves, and concealing their unhappiness at home by distracting themselves with complaints about work, family and children. On a positive note, some of them rediscovered their love for their husbands, and started turning a dull marriage into ones full of love, affection and complicity.

In the following section, I am sharing the story of a patient who has struggled for years with her parent-child and romantic relationships and was helped by past life therapy. In contrast to other cases in this book where the therapy duration was brief and outcomes swift, the duration of treatment in this case was long drawn.

THE CASE OF ALICE – INCAPACITY TO LOVE

In modern society the establishment of a couple relationship through emotional bonding is considered fundamental to happiness and wellbeing. However, in the presence of guilt feelings and affective disorders, specifically anxiety and depression, the ability to love another person can be severely hampered. In the case of Alice the use of regression therapy has helped her to unveil the root of the problem, and managed her life situation better.

Alice was a twenty-nine-year-old high school teacher, with blond curls falling along the side of her face. When she first came to my office, I noticed that she was always looking downwards with a mixture of anxiety and a sad look. She could have looked pretty had her appearance not been distorted by sadness and anguish. She told me that she had been experiencing depression since the age of fourteen. She had experienced some major depressive episodes and was now concerned with her chronic dysthymic mood[13] associated with chronic generalized anxiety. During her anxiety crises, she would feel desperate, not knowing what to do, and be suffused with deep anguish and somatic sensations, like shortness of breath and palpitations. She had tried many different medications and psychotherapy regimens, and was presently taking one antipsychotic and two antidepressant pills each day. This was in addition to the psychoanalytic therapy that she had been undergoing in the past two years.

In the first month, we managed her with medication and talked about her problems, while she continued to receive psychoanalytic therapy. She explained that the main difficulty she was facing was her interpersonal relationship with her mother, but more so with men in general. Somehow, she felt incapable of establishing any kind of relationship with adult men, not even ordinary or work-related friendships. The only man she managed to establish and maintain some long-term contact with was an uncle who lived in another state in Brazil, about 1800 kilometers away. However, even with this uncle she had disagreements, and that boosted her anxiousness.

Alice attributed her relationship difficulty to two earlier events in her life: her mother's reaction to divorce when she was four years old, and her frustrating experience with her first boyfriend who had erectile dysfunction. This latter event had led her to place on herself the feeling of being "impotent" in her failure to satisfy a man.

Alice's mother was a disturbed woman who had shielded herself from her own guilt feelings by deciding that no man could be trustworthy. She believed that a clever woman should stay

---

[13] Dysthymia – the word is of Greek origin. It is a mood disorder with the same cognitive and physical problems as in depression, but with less severe and longer-lasting symptoms.

away from men. At the same time, she exhorted her two daughters, Alice being the elder of the two, to find a good man each and marry, as a kind of "solution" or even "obligation" for a woman.

After four months of initial treatment, Alice made up her mind to start therapy with me, using hypnosis and regression.

Session 1: Witnessing Parents' Wedding

In her first session, Alice went into a relaxed state easily, and thereafter I guided her to establish a safe place for herself. For a troubled individual like her, a sense of safety and the process of building a secure frame in which therapy could take place were of paramount importance. She needed a secure environment to develop the necessary self-awareness and self-esteem to make sense of her experiences. This secure environment contained by our therapeutic relationship was the psychic space in which healing could take place.

Next, she established a "protection figure", which was really a symbolic personality whose role was to guard her safety and to whom she referred as her "angel friend".

Soon after entering a trance state, Alice regressed back to her childhood. She started to experience feelings of loneliness and unexplained guilt for her parents' divorce, as well as being responsible for her younger sister's wellbeing. I continued to guide her to go further back in time, until she could visualize her parents' marriage ceremony.

Alice visualized herself as a four-year-old girl witnessing her parents' wedding at the church. She felt anguished because no one in the church could see or hear her; nor could she get anybody's attention. When the ceremony ended and her parents were leaving the church, she stood on the stairs crying.

At the next scene, she was at her home's gate, and the wedding car with her newly married parents arrived. They got out of the car, passed by her, and again they neither saw nor heard her. This exaggerated her feelings of loneliness and abandonment.

As we integrated this regression experience together after she came out of trance, she was skeptical of this visual imagery. Coming from a background of Protestant Christianity[14], what she visualized was incompatible with her belief system. She argued logically that since she was conceived only after her parents married and born nine months later, it would be impossible for her to be physically present at the wedding ceremony.

Later, when she checked with her mother on the facts and went through the parents' wedding album, she saw some of the photographs matched with the scenes she had visualized under hypnotic regression. With this, she was then able to accept cryptomnesia[15] as a possible explanation for what she had seen. I then attempted to help her reframe her lonely and guilty feelings, but at that time her "angel friend" revealed that it was still impossible for her to get rid of her guilt.

Next, we spent some time discussing her present relationships. Soon, it was evident that whenever she got interested in a man, she would hastily jump into a physical and sexual relationship. Every time, that would turn out to be disastrous. The man would get what he wanted and quickly leave her alone thereafter.

Session 2: Past Life Leticia – Romance and Betrayal
The second regression brought Alice back to the life of a woman called Leticia who lived in a medium-sized city in south-eastern Brazil in the mid-twentieth century.

She visualized a scene of herself as a girl swaying in a garden swing, and a boy was noted to pass by frequently. One day, the boy stopped by, talked to her and appeared friendly. She was then excited with what she thought was the beginning of a romance.

---

[14] The dominant religion of Brazil was, and still is, Christianity.

[15] Cryptomnesia is a memory bias whereby a person experiences a previously forgotten memory as a new idea, thought or inspiration.

From that moment onwards, she waited every day for him to come. However, the boy never returned. Disappointed, she became wary of getting involved in romantic love ever since.

In that lifetime, Leticia lived only with her grandfather, who died while she was still a teenager, leaving her alone in the house.

 After growing up, she got herself a job as a kindergarten teacher, and her days passed monotonously with the same daily routine. She would leave her home with her books in the morning with her head looking downwards, and walk to work without talking to anyone along the way. At the workplace, she would barely exchange a couple of words with the headmaster. She only took care of the kids, and even with them she hardly spoke. By afternoon, she would pick up her books, walk home with her head looking down again and without talking to anyone.

On her way home one day, with her eyes fixed on the ground, she ran into a bicycle rider. As she reached out to help the young man whom she had knocked down, she was astonished that she immediately fell in love with him. While she did not know who this man was at that moment, the same individual appeared at a subsequent regression (Session 4), and was somebody whom she could identify with in her current life. With the start of the romance she changed her outlook. She was happy to be in love with him for some time, and eventually they decided to get married.

At the next scene, she visualized herself at a church ceremony with a beautiful wedding dress. Unfortunately, her fiancé never showed up. She waited for a long time until the people attending the ceremony started to leave. It was heart-breaking. Feeling lonely and dejected, and with no one to give her the needed emotional support, she went home, tore her wedding gown off violently and stepped on it. She shouted aloud that she would never trust any man, nor ever marry again. Then, speaking to God, she swore she would never go to church anymore. With that, she cried bitterly, took her car out and drove right in front of a moving truck and died instantly from the crash.

After she emerged from trance, Alice was astounded with the regression experience. While we were integrating the experience, she exclaimed, "How could all this be possible when I don't believe in reincarnation?"

"It could be a kind of fantasy which your own unconscious mind could have produced, to symbolize some things from your deep feelings," I explained.

"I can't believe it was a fantasy either, because it seemed too real!" she said.

Session 3: Past Life Lara – Low Esteem

Despite her disbelief, Alice continued with the therapy. In the next session, she regressed to a lifetime in Canada as Lara, a woman living with her mother and her aunt. It was a stressful lifetime. Both her mother and aunt were repeatedly putting her down, and incessantly criticizing her for doing things wrongly. Frustrated, she decided to shift out and move to another place that was chilly and snowy.

In that new place, Lara was involved with a married man and got pregnant. After her son was born, she became progressively depressed. So, she brought her baby to a place where her mother could find him. After that, she committed suicide by taking an overdose of medication.

While we were integrating this experience, she highlighted that the cold place and the moral issue of having an affair with a married man had added up to her feelings of guilt and uselessness, as a fundamental part of the depression.

As we continued, Alice visualized meeting her first boyfriend in her current life – the one that had the erection problem. This encounter made her very sad and desperate, and she felt unworthy of being loved. This feeling of being unloved remained unexplained though. She couldn't relate it to anything she knew, be it in her present life or in her previous regressions.

In the next regression scene, she saw herself differently as a rich, elegant woman, but harsh and lonely. The name of that woman that came to her mind at the moment was Maria Madalena. This name was associated with the impression of some deeply rooted guilt, of which she was unable to get rid. She did not know what the guilt was about, but she found herself incapable of forgiving herself. Hypnotically, Alice was unable to go further into that lifetime, and the session ended shortly afterwards. However, when she subsequently had the opportunity to explore her life as Maria Madalena again (in Session 5), she could obtain a better understanding of herself.

Session 4: Past Life Karina – Infidelity

At the next session three weeks later, Alice regressed again to yet another lifetime. This time she saw herself as Karina, a young woman living in the Brazilian colonial period. She was forced by her father to marry a much older man who was a rich farmer. She was unhappy, but she accepted it because that kind of marriage arrangement was common practice at the time.

After marriage, Karina established a good relationship with the black slaves, and after some years she started an affair with one of them. For this particular slave, she described him as being "not as dark as the others". She recalled some scenes in which she had secret meetings with her lover at a hidden place with a pond and a beautiful waterfall.

One day, her husband found out about her affair with the slave and sent his foremen to catch them while they were together. At the sight of the men coming, her lover promptly said sorry to her and indicated that he couldn't afford to stay on and wait to be caught. He ran away before the men came, while she stayed. The foremen brought her to her husband, who was furious and kicked her out of the home. From that moment onwards, she became very bitter.

Karina subsequently settled in another city, started working and eventually became rich. She became a landowner herself, and then started ill-treating her slaves. She died alone and unhappy at an old age. Still in a trance state, she suddenly recognized that the slave with whom she had an affair was the same man who had abandoned her (as Leticia) in a previous life at the marriage altar (Session 2). He was also the same individual as her subsequent boyfriend in her current lifetime. (Session 6)

This therapy session had brought on marked clinical progress. Alice appeared significantly improved when she came for her next session. She adopted a better attitude towards other people now, especially towards her friends and family members. Other people had noticed a change in her and her actions were more appropriate to the situations she encountered.

Two weeks later, she reported having spontaneous visions of the baby whom she had, as Lara in her past life, given birth to. Intuitively, she recognized the baby as one of her present life cousins, as if she was seeing him from the spiritual vantage point as Lara. For this reason, I took the opportunity to regress her back again to Lara's past life.

While reliving Lara's past life, she saw Lara's mother mistreating the boy and spanking him. This caused her to feel guilty and desperate, because she could not protect him. We went through a therapy process of releasing her guilt and sorrow, through reframing the experience and leaving space for her own good actions in the present lifetime.

After a further couple of months, Alice experienced further clinical improvement. However, at this point she had to bravely face some difficult situations at work and at home.

Session 5: Past Life Maria Madalena – Sexual Abuse
During this session, she went again into the lifetime of that rich, harsh woman called Maria Madalena.

This time she visualized the early life of Maria Madalena as a sweet girl until her teenage years. She re-experienced a disturbing conversation with a friend at that time. She strongly argued her view for the importance and existence of love, while her friend disdained of love, saying it was a farce.

Soon afterwards, still as a teenager, her foster father began to sexually abuse her, and she was kept for some time as his "lover". Feeling filthy and disgusted, she decided that love really didn't exist after all. Her attitude changed, and she subsequently got married to a rich and disgusting old man, focusing only on his wealth and social status. While she was successful in the material aspect, she became that bitter and harsh woman whom she saw earlier towards the end of Session 3.

We integrated all these experiences, and Alice had some good insights from her regressions. I worked with her in the trance state to cleanse her feelings of filth and disgust. With the help of her "angel friend" and the imagery of a healing light, she was led towards being more self-forgiving and a happy state.

The following few months did not bring the clinical improvement as expected. In fact Alice was seen to be a little more anxious and impatient. She recalled some things about her childhood, and stated that she had absolutely no good memories of her early years at all. She was tired, overworked, and wanted to slow down on her therapy because she was going through a rough time financially. As it was around mid-December, we decided to take a break for a month to coincide with her vacation.

Session 6: Back to Past Life Karina

Resting did her good. When we resumed therapy after the break, Alice was feeling much better. She was even showing signs of being close to a boyfriend, whom she did not consider handsome, but sensitive and understanding. Nevertheless, there was still a long way to go on her part because the thought of the possibility of having a relationship with him still made her anorexic.

At this session, she went into a new regression experience and she was led to review the lifetime as Karina in which she had an affair with the slave (Session 4). Surprisingly, she now recognized the slave as the same individual as her boyfriend in her present life. She remembered that she had become very angry at him during that previous lifetime, because she expected him to have stood by her side when her husband discovered their affair. Instead, the slave, afraid that he would lose his life if caught, ran away and disappointed her. So, she had made a conscious decision never again to love a man, and never again to believe in love. This reinforced the similar decisions she had made in other lifetimes and those decisions were hard to give up.

Alice's therapy continued, alternating between work in trance state and cognitive therapy. There was a mix of different therapeutic approaches, from the more direct, cognitive-behavioral approach to a broader, transpersonal approach.

Interestingly, her boyfriend managed to become a romantic partner for a short period of about three months. Thereafter she continued to progress slowly in her emotional wellbeing, towards acquiring a more mature and conscious attitude of herself.

Recovery

The path to recovery was not a smooth one. Alice continued to experience attacks of anxiety during which she felt uneasy, and sometimes with the fear that she could not cope with her stress. She even thought about suicide, but fortunately each time the thought arose, she promptly rejected the idea.

A couple of years later, Alice witnessed two car accidents within the same week. That reminded her of the regression experience as Leticia (Session 2) during which she killed herself with a deliberate car crash and as Lara (Session 3) in the lifetime where she committed suicide after giving birth. The recollection of the memory of her suffering associated with the suicides in those previous lifetimes had helped her to make a strong, conscious decision to never take away her own life again.

This had been an unusual case with the severity of the problem and the patient needing far longer to integrate the therapy sessions into her current life. While most regression therapy would require sessions over a few months, with Alice it extended over a period of about nine years.

The interval between Alice's sessions had ranged from a few months to more than a year. During these times Alice still had to deal with many aspects of her own insecurity. This included the management of her relationship with her difficult mother, and learning to improve her relationships with men through trial and error. During this journey, she had several flashbacks of her previous lifetimes. With the details recalled, she could integrate them and even elucidate some issues and insights on her own. In fact, in one regression experience, she went back again to her present childhood, to work with her feelings of guilt about her parents' divorce.

It was a long journey. She had lots of issues to deal with and lots of experiences and feelings to process. My role as the therapist was to walk alongside her, support her emotionally and help her get in touch with her deeper self and the reality of her inner world.

Breakthrough

Our efforts eventually paid off. Alice gradually began developing different relationships with her friends and romantic partners. She was in the process of becoming aware that men were also human with both positive and negative qualities, and learning how to deal with their shortcomings. Almost eight years after our first session, she took a major step forward. She moved out from her mother's home!

Next, I realized she had been dating the same man for a couple of years. That was a remarkable improvement compared to how she was struggling with love when she first came to me. She was happy with the man, even though she felt he was not as smart and dedicated to professional growth to the same extent as she was. At one point, they were thinking of moving in to stay together, but she decidedly refused that, because she wanted to have the experience of living alone and taking care of herself. Slightly more than one year later, they married.

That was a breakthrough!

At the wedding ceremony, while they were exchanging their marital vows, I heard her saying distinctly to her marriage partner: "Thank you, for being such a loving man, and most of all, thank you for making me believe again that love exists!" Following those words, Alice turned her head smilingly to one side and looked straight at me. There was a clear signal in her expression.

It was a most meaningful and a memorable moment. Behind the achievement was the story of a flaming heart within. If it hadn't been for those long hard years of struggle with her therapy, I would never have felt that sense of accomplishment.

Concluding Thoughts

Alice's story is a complex one, as are most of the stories we encounter in therapy, especially in the presence of associated depression and panic disorder. It is after all, about handling the relationships we have in various lifetimes, dealing with different situations, but always facing the difficult task of living with people that are necessarily different from us. We need to learn to love, and to be loved.

Alice was repeating the same pattern lifetime after lifetime. Her problem was that she felt guilty for something she had done in one of her past lives and that feeling of guilt prevented her from being happy in subsequent lifetimes. She refused to love, then tried again, but always had her expectation frustrated. This resulted in self-destruction and a renewed decision to never love again.

When we went back further, she located the source of that pattern as having come from her lifetime as Maria Madalena. Her revolt against being abused by her foster father had resulted in a harsh and mean attitude throughout that lifetime. This had generated a long-lasting guilty feeling.

In the present lifetime, she had an unexplained guilt about her childhood experience pertaining to the unloving parent-parent and parent-daughter relationships. As a child, Alice undeservingly took the guilt upon herself. This is not unusual because, as children, we usually believe our parents are perfect. If and when something goes wrong at home, we tend to blame ourselves, as we know we are not perfect.

As an epilogue, Alice came back to my office for a couple of times a few months after her marriage, and it was to deal with some minor problems related to her work. I followed up with her clinical condition four years later. She had weaned off all psychiatric medication and felt really happy. By then, she was more mature and independent, and had not experienced any major episode of anxiety or depression.

PART THREE

Medical Illnesses

CHAPTER SIX

Body Therapy for Refractory Asthma

Dr. Moacir Oliveira

"At the very instant that you think 'I am happy', a chemical messenger translates your emotion, which has no solid existence whatever in the material world, into a bit of matter so perfectly attuned to your desire that literally every cell in your body learns of your happiness and joins in."

Dr. Deepak Chopra, MD
In: Quantum Healing, 1990.

y path towards regression therapy has been a gradual one. I graduated from medical school in 1985 and took up specialty training in Psychiatry in Salvador, Brazil. In the course of my practice, I stumbled upon clinical situations in which I felt dissatisfied with the effectiveness of conventional methods of treatment, including their adverse effects. Thereafter, in my search for alternative therapies, I looked out for modalities that offered more personal autonomy and were more compatible with patients' values and beliefs on the nature and meaning of health and disease.

My Journey as Therapist

I first came across transpersonal psychology[16] at the Bahia School of Medicine and Public Health in Salvador, Brazil, in 2003 at a specialization course. It was a stimulating experience and during this course, I got to know the work of the late Roger Woolger (1944–2011). He was a Jungian analyst by training and had produced some of the most influential works in the field of regression therapy. He came to Brazil in 2005 to conduct a workshop on past life therapy. At that time, I was already familiar with some of the teachings of Tibetan Buddhism and Spiritism of Allan Kardec[17] and was comfortable with the concept of reincarnation. Hence, I had no problem aligning my belief system with the use of past life therapy in the treating of clinical problems that were related to traumatic events in the patient's previous lives. After all, some of these symptoms had already been classified as "psychosomatic" in medicine. Soon, I discovered that the use of regression therapy in such situations could lead to substantial relief and rapid recovery.

I trained with Roger Woolger during the period 2005–07 in Brazil. In his training, Roger introduced the approach of working with the body with the concept that "the body tells its own story." This was appealing to me. He also combined the use of body psychotherapy with psychodrama to release the traumatic memories that were embedded in particular parts of the patient body and had been frozen. I found that fascinating.

---

[16] Transpersonal psychology deals with those experiences in which the sense of self extends beyond the individual to include wider aspects of life, humankind, psyche and the cosmos. It considers issues of self-development, peak experiences, altered states of consciousness and the expanded experiences of living.

[17] Allan Kardec (1804–69), a French teacher, was raised as a Catholic and known for his work in systematizing Spiritism. He believed in reincarnation and published his first book *The Spirits' Book* in 1857.

When I first used regression technique on patients with symptoms that were non-responsive to conventional medicine, I encountered pleasant surprises. The results were distinctly positive and the healing responses were both rapid and dramatic.

In this chapter, I am sharing my personal experience of a patient with refractory asthma, whose journey through regression therapy was both awesome and inspiring.

THE CASE OF MARY – BRONCHIAL ASTHMA

Bronchial asthma is a chronic disease characterized by airway inflammation. When an attack occurs, the lining of the walls of the bronchial air passages are swollen, while the muscles surrounding the airways tighten. As a result, the air passages go into spasm and the amount of air that can flow into the lungs is drastically reduced. Often, the attack is promptly reversible with bronchodilators and steroid treatment.

Asthma is a problem of public health worldwide because of its prevalence and the high socioeconomic costs involved in treatment. The maintenance of an asthma-free state in the individual depends on the action of various external factors in the environment, especially if the individual is genetically predisposed. From the clinical viewpoint, asthma is a multifaceted disorder that is varied in its clinical manifestations and natural history, requiring a careful, comprehensive inter- and multi-disciplinary approach in its treatment.

Of concern is a subgroup of severe asthmatics that remain poorly controlled, despite high doses of inhaled and oral corticosteroids. My patient, Mary, is one such example. Such patients are generally known to have a greater morbidity and a need for greater health care support.

Initial Visit

Mary was a fifty-eight-year-old lady of thin build, short stature and with black hair. She turned up at my office on 10 June 2011 with her husband and was seeking help for her asthmatic condition. When I first saw her, she was breathing normally, speaking softly and slowly, and appeared calm.

I soon found out that Mary had been suffering from bronchial asthma since 1994, the year when her father died. After several attacks, she sought the advice of a respiratory physician who performed a clinical evaluation and a battery of investigations. The latter included chest radiography, spirometry, allergy testing, nasopharyngoscopy and bronchoscopy, but unfortunately the results were unhelpful towards solving her problem. She was prescribed with bronchodilators and corticosteroids and underwent physiotherapy. She was taught breathing exercises and techniques of cough control and mucus removal. She also tried hydrotherapy to help her loosen nasal secretions, cleanse nasal passages and improve bronchial drainage. She even went through cognitive behavioral therapy, to learn to reduce her anxiety and the panic associated with her asthmatic attacks. However, none of these measures helped.

Her condition worsened, and at one point Mary was experiencing the asthmatic attacks daily. She felt desperate because no treatment seemed to help. On two occasions she developed cardiorespiratory arrest as a result of the attacks, but was fortunately resuscitated in time.

"I continued to suffer, while repeatedly paying visits to various doctors and hospitals and buying modern inhalers, but none of them worked. I kept spending my nights barely breathing and without sleep," Mary recounted in dismay.

As I listened to her story, I felt a sense of dread and uneasiness, wondering if her problem was within my scope of expertise.

"As a last attempt, I tried getting the help from a respiratory physician in Salvador-Bahia," she recalled. "He said I had a narrowing of the passage of the larynx and the trachea is flattened. That was why I had such severe asthma and would need corrective surgery!"

Mary was shocked with this last assessment. It left her dumbfounded and in a state of confusion as to whether she should follow this physician's advice on the recommended course of action. However, she did not give up hope.

"One day, my sister brought to my attention that there is a physician who performs past life regression therapy," Mary said. "She suggested that I may want to come to you to explore this treatment approach. That's why I am here today."

It felt good to hear of her trust in me, but I hesitated to offer treatment because of other considerations. Clearly, her asthmatic condition was refractory in nature. While I felt a deep desire to help, I was equally cognizant of the possible complications that could arise during the therapy. With a severe asthmatic like her, the processing of emotions that might arise during hypnotic regression could precipitate a crisis of bronchospasm and lead to serious consequences.

After some thought, I reassured her that I would work out a treatment plan, and then gave her an appointment to return the following week, by which time I should be better prepared. In the meanwhile I arranged for an oxygen tank and mask and a resuscitative trolley equipped with the necessary emergency medication to be made available in my office. It was a precautionary measure that I couldn't afford to overlook.

Session 1: Past Life as Slave

Mary turned up promptly on 16 June 2011 for her first therapy session. She appeared anxious on arrival.

I reminded myself to be extra cautious in handling her case. After putting her at ease, I spent some time allaying her fears while persuading her to relax on a reclining couch. With six years of experience in regression therapy behind me, I displayed my confidence as I reassured her that everything would be in control during the session.

After our initial dialogue, Mary appeared calmer. I then instructed her to close her eyes and guided her through three deep, slow breaths. However, at the end of her third breath, her nervousness surfaced and began to escalate. There were signs of mounting restlessness and I noticed some difficulty in her breathing. I reminded myself to be patient. Without causing any alarm, I asked her gently, "How are you feeling now?"

"My chest cannot expand," she replied, sounding anxious. "I'm finding it difficult to breathe."

After a quick evaluation, I concluded that she was not about to initiate an asthmatic attack. Rather, she was connecting herself with a frozen body memory, because I sensed that her body was struggling to tell her a story of her past, which was related to her asthmatic condition. Riding on the opportunity, I applied a formal hypnotic induction technique and quickly got her into a trance state. Once under trance, I directed Mary's attention to her chest.

"What prevents your chest from expanding?" I asked.

"Something is squeezing my body," Mary replied, with her eyes remaining closed.

In my mind, the opportune moment seemed to have arrived!

It is a fundamental principle of body psychotherapy[18] that muscular tension reflects a repressed emotion. When this emotion is harnessed in some way, it can be conveniently used as an affect bridge. I seized the opportunity and asked Mary to focus on her body tightness, and this maneuver connected her immediately with a past life.

"Tell me who you are and what you see," I prompted.

"I am a black female, approximately twenty-five years old; slim in shape and with black hair. I'm lying on the floor with my arms tied together by a rope to my body," she said. It sounded very much a lifetime in which Mary was a slave.

As her description became more vivid, her breathlessness also increased. I waited patiently for more story details to emerge.

After a pause she said, "I'm dying."

Her shortness of breath worsened as she was describing her dying scene in that life. Concerned that her breathlessness may deteriorate further, I intervened quickly to halt the symptom progression without getting her out of trance.

I said to Mary that I would be snapping my fingers in a moment, and when I did so her heart would have stopped completely and she would be out of the death experience by then.

"One, two, and three. Now ..." I snapped my fingers, and paused for a moment.

"Tell me what happened after all your energies left your body?"

I noticed that Mary's rate of breathing had suddenly slowed down.

"I'm calm," she said. "My body is now stagnant; it's not moving."

---

[18] Body psychotherapy was founded by Wilhelm Reich and became popular in the 1960s and 1970s but was not considered part of mainstream psychoanalytic therapy.

"What are your thoughts now?"

"I am free … I no longer have to submit myself to that tedious job, day after day and non-stopping. I am very tired of myself in that situation."

I asked why she was tied up in that manner. She told me that she had felt tired and refused to work. Hence she faced punishment as a result. She was then tied up and dragged to the sugar cane fields. It was clear that her past life as a black slave was harsh.

Slavery in Brazil began in the first half of the sixteenth century, with the growth of the sugar cane industry. The Portuguese colonizers had brought black slaves from their established colonies in Africa to use as slave labor in the sugar plantations. Many of these slaves were kidnapped from their homeland in North Africa from areas including present-day Angola, Mozambique and the Democratic Republic of Congo. Flogging was one of the more commonly used methods of intimidation and physical punishment, because it guaranteed work and obedience. Slavery lasted for more than three hundred years in Brazil, until it was officially abolished with the signing of the Golden Law in 1888.

As the therapy continued, I asked Mary if there was something that had not been resolved in that lifetime.

"The strings on my body remain tight. They are restricting my chest and preventing me from breathing normally," she said.

In my training in regression therapy, Roger Woolger had always encouraged his students to assemble a kit to be ready for use in case psychodrama was needed. Such a kit would consist of ropes, fabrics, wood chips or any objects that could help to simulate the tactile memory of different kinds of trauma on the physical body. So in Mary's case, I took out a piece of rope from my kit and simulated her past life situation by tying her arms and her chest with it.

Next, I gradually loosened and untied the ropes under trance as I directed her attention to the feeling of a return of her body strength, while she continued to visualize the imagery of the ropes being untied and removed. This allowed her to experience the feeling of the sudden release of chest tightness. This was an effective technique that we often used.

In this approach, the therapy model assumes that the body holds the echoes of traumatic incidents and abuse. By paying attention to the patient's unexpressed reflexes, these frozen memories can be released from the body. The maneuver involves the allowing of the completion of the patient's unfulfilled desires or held-back impulses.

I repeated the procedure until Mary was brought to her consciousness that, whatever had been holding her back in her past life, was now gone. She now felt free from the restraint. She was breathing freer and easier after this procedure was completed.

"Is there something else that is unfinished?" I resumed.

"No, there isn't. I understand that I didn't want to work. It was his right to insist that I work. As a slave, I should not disobey," she said.

After these words, Mary relaxed into a deep sleep. Her breathing had normalized and I left her alone to rest. Twenty minutes later, she woke up by herself, looking calm and peaceful and remarked, "I am feeling very tired, but now that my chest is freed, I can breathe and sleep well."

Session 2: Past Life as a Slave Executioner

There was a significant improvement after the first therapy session. Since then, Mary could breathe much better and sleep through the night without medication. She returned a fortnight later, on 1 July, feeling happy and looking forward to a second therapy session.

Positioned on the couch with her eyes closed, she was eager to proceed with the therapy. It was encouraging. However, as I began to guide her to relax, I noticed she started to display the same breathing difficulty as in her previous session.

"How are you feeling, Mary?" I asked.

She coughed, and said she experienced a feeling of something around her neck. Fortunately, being an easily hypnotizable patient, she continued to slide into a trance state.

"Doctor, there's a rope around my neck, I'm being hanged," she said. I realized that Mary had gone straight into another past life following my short induction.

"Hanged?" I asked with surprise.

"Yes, this time I am a white and strong man, about thirty-five years of age. I am clothed in thick fabric and wearing boots."

Mary continued to cough and began to feel more breathless. To avoid this from escalating into an attack of bronchospasm, I quickly asked her to go to the most important and crucial moment of that story.

"One, two and three ..." I snapped my fingers and asked her to move forward in time.

Mary's body shuddered. There were some twitching movements following which she appeared relaxed. Her breathing slowed down and the rhythm became more regular.

"How do you feel now?" I asked.

"I still feel a pressure on my throat. It hurts and there seems to be an object right in front of my neck."

At this point, I took out a rope, put it around her neck and applied a slight pressure. In response to this stimulation, she began to squirm and feel breathless again. I encouraged her to calm down, and suggested to her to use her own hands to remove the rope. There was some initial resistance to my suggestion, but after some hesitation, Mary managed to complete the action with difficulty, and gave a sigh of relief.

She relaxed for a few minutes and I checked on her feeling once again.

"I am peaceful," she said. "There's only a slight discomfort on my neck now."

Suddenly, Mary understood why her past life self was in that condition and experiencing that sensation. "I am an executioner of slaves. When they do not obey me and do not want to work, I torture them. I put them in the torture place and use the whip to punish them. They learn fast."

"What are your feelings when you punish the slaves?"

"None ... I am only taking orders from the lord of the mill."

"And what is the reason that you are being hanged?"

"Some time ago, I fell in love with one of the slaves, and I have maintained that relationship with her since. The work in the farm is very intense. One day, she fell sick and couldn't work. My boss ordered me to punish her for not working, but I disobeyed. He was angry; hit me for my disobedience and I retaliated. So the lord of the mill sent the other executioners to hang me."

"What do you feel about the lord of the mill?" I asked.

"I deserve the punishment because I have disobeyed his orders. This is the law. Whoever doesn't obey will have to pay with his life ... and I paid."

At this point I noticed that her eyes were filled with tears. I then asked, "Is there anything else pending?"

"Yes ... I miss her."

"You mean the slave with whom you fell in love?" I asked.

"Yes."

I then brought Mary to complete her transition through the death point.

"What is happening now?"

"They take my body and bury it in the bush. I see a light ... a strong white light is approaching me. I feel the heat from the light. I feel well and peaceful."

"Look at the light, and see who is showing up?"

At this point Mary went into catharsis.

"She's here .... she hugs me and says she will stay with me." I understood that Mary was referring to the slave lover. I then offered her a cushion to hug, as if it was her slave friend. This is another technique of psychodrama[19] that is commonly used in regression therapy to simulate an emotional encounter.

A few minutes lapsed. Mary's emotion settled down, and I decided to bring her out of trance. "How do you feel now?" I asked.

"I feel calm and peaceful. I can breathe freely now," she said.

"Good job you did in this session." I praised her for her cooperation. I offered her a glass of water and helped her to sit up.

It was increasingly obvious that Mary was on her way to recovery. However, I reminded her that she would need to continue the treatment. "Although you are now off medication, your treatment with regression therapy is incomplete. You'll still need a couple of therapy sessions more to clear your residual tension," I said.

With that, I gave her another appointment a fortnight's time.

---

[19] Psychodrama is a way of investigating the human soul through action created by Jacob Levy Moreno. It is a method of intervention in interpersonal relationships and facilitates the search for alternatives to the resolution of what is revealed.

Session 3: Past Life as a Jewish Woman

Mary remained well and had been breathing normally. She continued to sleep well in the night and had been going to the beach for sunbathing. In fact, she had been free of asthmatic attacks since.

She returned on 15 July. Once again, I got her to close her eyes after she positioned herself on the couch. Like before, I guided her through three deep breaths. This time, at the completion of her third breath, she again started coughing like in her second session. In addition, she also experienced a choking sensation.

"I'm dying," Mary suddenly shouted.

I was startled, but as she seemed to be in trance, I suspected that she was just about to connect with another past life.

"Tell me more," I said.

"I'm being suffocated by smoke," she said.

Panting, Mary told me that she was a woman of twenty-five years old in that lifetime, with white skin and black hair. What I had not expected was that she was back to the biblical times then!

Mary described herself as being inside a house that was set on fire by King Herod's soldiers. She was busy trying to save her two-year-old son from the calamity. As it turned out, she was referring to the Massacre of the Innocents, an act of infanticide ordered by King Herod of Judea. This incident was described in the Gospel of Matthew[20]. Herod had ordered the execution of all the boys in the village of Bethlehem to avoid losing the throne to the newborn "King of the Jews", whose birth had been revealed to him by the Three Wise Men.

"Son ... the house is on fire!" she yelled emotionally.

---

[20] The Massacre was described in Matthew 2:16–18. The Gospel of Matthew is the first book of the New Testament and one of the four canonical gospels.

I immediately passed her a pillow and she embraced it as if she was holding her child. However, her breathing turned increasingly rapid.

I next moved her story forward to the point when the massacre ended. She relaxed and returned gradually to normal breathing. However, she remained hugging the pillow firmly and appeared to be in sorrow. I waited for a few minutes for her to settle down. Then she passed me back the pillow and said, "We died together."

"What happened?" I asked.

"When we died, I saw a bright light appearing and approaching us. It came close and it appeared as if a white mist had enveloped us. I felt a lot of peace then .... I'm fine now."

After emerging from trance, Mary was visibly touched by what she had visualized. To my knowledge as a therapist, the imagery of "white light" is a gentle but powerful energy for healing. For some reason, Mary did not want to talk about it. She indicated she needed solace at this point.

We agreed to schedule another time when we could talk more comfortably and perhaps integrate this past life experience. She said goodbye and left in silence.

Integration of Past Life Selves

Mary returned eight days later to update me of her progress. Upon entering the room she apologized and explained why she had left immediately towards the end of the previous session, avoiding the debrief.

"I was very moved by the presence of a bright light and the appearance of a white mist. I felt an increased awareness of myself, a sense of peace and a feeling of general wellbeing within me. And at that moment, I felt as if I was in the presence of God himself. I was very excited and exuberant and I wanted to maintain my silence until I had internalized my healing experience."

I listened carefully without comment. Instead, I asked if she still suffered from the lack of air in her breathing. To this she replied that she had suffered no asthmatic crisis since she started the therapy with me.

It was gratifying to hear her response. However, I still felt that some sort of integration of the experiences from her previous session was needed. At that point, I suggested to her that I could enable her to make contact with her past life characters using a Gestalt technique.[21] She nodded in agreement.

First, I put four chairs in a circle and asked Mary to sit in one of them. Then I asked her to close her eyes and relax. "Now imagine that sitting in those three chairs facing you are the three characters of your past lives," I began.

"Visualize their presence ..." I allowed some time for her to enter into a meditative state. Then I continued, "when you are ready, I want you to describe each one of them to me."

As the imagery of her past life selves emerged, Mary started talking. "In the first chair sits a slave woman. She is smiling, and

---

[21] Gestalt therapy is a phenomenological-existential therapy founded by Frederick and Laura Perls in the 1940s. The objective is to enable the patient to be more fully and creatively alive and free from blocks.

looks curious and happy. She has loose hair and is wearing a white dress."

It sounded as if Mary was already in a trance state.

"In the second chair sits a strong man of thirty-five years. He is white, and is smiling. In the third chair, there is a young woman, twenty-five years of age, with a two-year-old boy on her lap."

"Well done, Mary. Next, I want you to talk to them," I said.

This was another example of psychodrama in which role playing and guided drama is used to work through one's problems. After some moments of dialogue exchange with her past life selves, Mary made a startling comment.

"I now realize how my illness makes sense in my life. I understand why I have been handicapped for nearly eighteen years and suffering from breathing difficulties," she exclaimed.

Next, she spoke to her past life selves, "I keep reliving the moments of my physical death for you. My body and I understand that the life of each one of you existed in another time-line and place. However, my body does not know how to distinguish between time and space, and has kept in memory the death moment of each of the three of you."

This was profound insight. I remained silent and allowed her to continue.

"After a few sessions with past life regression therapy, I have since reprogrammed my body, and it now knows that all three of you have lived in the past, and henceforth you are free. I feel good now. I know I will not have any more asthmatic attacks henceforth. We're all free!"

There was an air of finality. At this point, Mary visualized, in a fascinating manner, how her past life characters rose up from their chairs and vanished into thin air.

I ended the session by reassuring Mary that everything would be fine. I offered to review her at six-monthly intervals but she politely declined. This was because she was residing in another city and travelling to my clinic for regular reviews would be inconvenient. Instead, we agreed to stay in touch through e-mail.

Concluding Thoughts

Six months later, Mary sent me a delightful message:

"Dear Doctor,

I'm now fine and my asthmatic attacks are totally gone. My pulmonologist has discharged me medically. I recall my first visit to your clinic on 10 June 2011 and it has been six months since. I am happy to say that I have found my life again. I have asked the Lord to disseminate my story to all doctors that this form of treatment is available for cases where conventional Medicine does not give the desired results. I never had a proper night's sleep for the past 18 years because of this disease. However, with just five clinic visits including three sessions of past life therapy, I have now understood the root of my illness. I'm so grateful for your help."

As I reflected over this case, I made a note that Mary's pulmonary reactivity to her asthma had initially worsened upon the death of her father. She began to have frequent bronchospasm, because the body memory of her own past life deaths had been awakened. The use of past life therapy had brought to light the experiences embedded in her body. Indeed, one of the remarkable aspects of this therapy is to keep the focus on the body to unfreeze its stored memories.

The body is where the physical violence of the individual's past and the associated emotions are most vividly experienced and recorded. Our body carries a record of not only our developmental history of the present life, but also the trauma of our past life histories. The symptom of breathing difficulty that Mary brought with her to the therapy had turned out to be the key to unlocking her frozen body energy. By simply encouraging her to live her past life stories, and creatively exploring the use of body therapy techniques, she was able to release her emotions physically and completely. The results in this case had been both dramatic and gratifying.

CHAPTER SEVEN

Past Life Origin of Chronic Pain

Dr. Moacir Oliveira

"A lot of people say they want to get out of pain, and I'm sure that's true, but they aren't willing to make healing a high priority. They aren't willing to look inside to see the source of their pain in order to deal with it."

Lindsay Wagner,
Holist Healer

Chronic pain syndrome is a major challenge in clinical Medicine because of its unclear etiology, complex natural history, poorly understood pathophysiology and a generally poor response to treatment. It may sometimes be a learned behavioral that starts with a pain stimulus and is rewarded by external attention from others or it may be caused by internal factors such as guilt.

One of the causes of diffuse musculoskeletal pain is that of *fibromyalgia*. The term refers to a chronic, painful condition where the pain is widespread. This condition is considered to be a disorder of pain processing due to abnormalities of pain-signal processing in the central nervous system. It predominantly affects women and is clinically characterized by a picture of pain, fatigue, malaise, sleep disturbances, mood swings and decreased physical activity. It is associated with the individual's sensitivity to a painful stimulus and can impair her quality of life and work performance. Several factors, alone or combined, may favor the manifestations of fibromyalgia, including serious illness, emotional or physical trauma, and hormonal changes. Apart from this, very little is known about the etiology of this disease.

In the following section I share the story of how the root of the pain of fibromyalgia has been successfully traced in one patient using regression therapy. This eventually enabled her to heal. Interestingly, the source of the pain was traced back to an origin in a previous lifetime.

THE CASE OF ANA – FIBROMYALGIA

Ana was a forty-three-year-old lady who was recommended by one of my colleagues to see me. She called me on my cellphone one day during my lunch break to ask for an appointment and eventually turned up in my office on the mid-morning of 20 January 2013.

Ana had been suffering from fibromyalgia with generalized body pain for several months. This had caused her much discomfort and difficulty with sleep. She had undergone both conventional and complementary treatments for her problem but had not experienced any significant improvement. As her treatment options were being exhausted she had recently sought the advice of a professional who worked with microphysiotherapy[22] and he suggested that she try the option of past life therapy.

---

[22] Microphysiotherapy is a holistic therapy that is based on the theory of the presence of energy links between different body structures belonging to the same embryological germ layer to explain the origin of symptoms that are otherwise incomprehensible and unrelated.

Ana was about 1.60 meters tall with thick brown hair. She communicated well and was open to sharing her thoughts and feelings in depth. She highlighted those areas of her body that had been badly affected by pain for more than eight months and unresponsive to treatment.

Ana used to work as a nurse in the city hospital. It was a good job with an attractive salary but she had since given it up because of the intensity of her symptoms. She liked her work, but couldn't keep up with the demands of the job because she had to cope with the severe pain and her sleepless nights. Of late, she had been consuming large quantities of pain-killers. As a result of the side effects, she had been constantly feeling sleepy and slow-witted during the day.

She had been married for four years but, as a sufferer of polycystic ovary disease, she had no children. Three years ago she lost her father, and ten months ago her mother also passed on. Currently, her pain seemed to have overwhelmed her life and career and got in the way of her living a fulfilling family and married life. In recent months, she had been through various alternative therapies including Bach flower remedies[23], chromotherapy[24] and Reiki[25] but the effects of these therapies were short-lived. Over the past year, when the pain had become very intense, she nearly lost the desire to live. She had been

---

[23] Bach flower remedies is a system of 38 flower therapies established by Dr. Edward Bach in 1936 which consists of extreme dilutions of flower material. The active ingredient is energy from the plant and not a physical substance, and it works by correcting emotional imbalance.
[24] Chromotherapy is a method of treatment that uses colors from the visible part of the electromagnetic spectrum to treat illnesses.
[25] Reiki is a form of stress reduction and energy healing conducted by laying of hands on the affected part of the body, based on the idea of a life force energy harvested from the cosmos.

taking antidepressant drugs and mood stabilizers as prescribed by her doctor, but these had not worked.

Session 1: Past Life as a Black Slave

It was 12 noon by the time I completed the initial interview with Ana. From the history given, I felt I had a good chance of helping her to heal.

Positioned comfortably on the therapy couch, I got Ana to go through a breathing exercise followed by a progressive muscular relaxation process that induced her into a trance state. Then I brought her attention back to her breath for a few moments, and guided her to imagine herself in a safe place where she would feel protected and secure.

The establishment of a safe place for therapy is an important preliminary step, in that the patient needs to feel supported when she expresses her many disturbing feelings and thoughts. It is a private, psychic space that can be easily created through visual imagery while the patient is entering the trance state.

Soon Ana described herself sitting comfortably on a sandy beach, relaxing and enjoying the serenity of the environment.

"Stay on the beach, and I want you to go back to the first time when you felt a lot of pain," I said.

I paused for a moment for her mental imagery to evolve. "Now, tell me the associated emotion that is emerging."

"Anger," she responded promptly.

An emotion emerging spontaneously in this manner often lends itself to being used as an affect bridge. This bridging technique involves the moving of a patient's consciousness exponentially from the present to a past event, over an affect that is common to both events. With the help of the therapist, the current affect can be vivified while the patient is asked to return to an earlier experience where the affect was felt.

"Focus on the anger. I'll help you to amplify it by counting from one to five, and at each count, you will double your pain level. One, two, three, four ... and five, and you now find yourself in a state of maximum intensity of anger. Next, I will be counting backwards from five to one. When I reach the count of one, you go back in time to an event when you experienced the same emotion in the same way."

This effect was immediate. Upon reaching the count of one, Ana went right back to a lifetime when she was a black slave working for a white master.

"My arms are being tied, and it hurts!" she began.

The scene was set in Brazil, and so the past life story did not come as a surprise. The whites that colonized the land depended heavily on indigenous labor to maintain the subsistence economy. Sugar was the primary export during the sixteenth-century and slave labor was the driving force behind the growth of the sugar economy. Many slaves were imported from Africa.

"There is a big-sized, white man who is carrying a whip in his hand," she continued. "I recognize him as the lord of the mill. He lashes me on my back with the whip. Oh ... it is painful and my back is bleeding a lot." She winced, and her trunk muscles tensed up.

"What are your thoughts then?" I asked.

"I am wondering ... why is this happening to me?"

"What emotions are associated with this thought?"

"Anger and stress," she said unhesitatingly.

"How do you feel now?"

"Angry." Ana's facial muscles tensed up. "I know I'm going to die. It's for the wrong reason. Things could have turned out differently ... but I hate giving in to what he wants." Ana's eyes were flickering.

"What does he want?"

"I keep thinking ... I will not let him do that to me. My body is very tense. I feel fearful ... because of the potential threat he poses to my family."

"What is the thought that goes with your fear?"

"I hate this. I am afraid of what is going to happen next. I also wonder if I can handle it." Ana's voice quivered with trepidation, and she seemed to be near to her threshold of tolerance. Instinctively, I knew I had to step in to moderate the situation.

"Yes, you can," I gently reassured her, and after a short pause, followed up with a question.

"What can possibly happen next? What is the reason behind what is happening to you right now?"

"I am being used as an example. It is a warning for other slave women against doing what I did ... I have hurt him."

"Tell me how you did that."

There was a pause as she struggled for words.

"I could visualize a white-walled room with a table inside. Next to the table is a bed. He pushed me on to the bed. I struggled, but he tore my clothes off." Ana's face turned pale. With some hesitation, she continued.

"He forced my legs and thighs apart." This gruesome description of a revolting action made Ana's voice sound ghastly. "I could see that he was totally naked. He wanted to rape me. I did not allow that to happen. I scratched his face and cut it with my nails. He retreated in shock ... his face was bleeding. In anger, he called the foreman into the room. He gave him the order to tie me to the torture stake and whip me." Her face was flushed as she tightened both her hands into fists.

"What happened next?"

"I remained tied to the torture stake for some time. My back was bleeding. He came back several times during the day to beat me up again in front of the other slaves. Everyone was witnessing the torture. With the blood-stained scarf held against his face, he shouted angrily at me that he was beating up a rotten and filthy woman."

"I was tired. My body withered under the heat of the sun and the pain of the whip. My vision became progressively clouded. In time, I was unable to see anything."

At that point I observed that several muscle groups were twitching on Ana's body. It was as if the body was trying to tell a story. I remembered from my training that muscle tension reflected repressed emotions.[26] This teaching was based on the concept that human beings developed fixed and rigid postures and patterns of relating as a means to protect themselves from emotional pain. I took the opportunity to deepen Ana's trance state and encouraged her to concentrate on her body.

"Focus on the sensations on your own body and tell me how you are feeling about it."

"It seems that my body is very rigid. I can't breathe anymore." Her voice sounded desperate.

"Imagine that you are stepping out of your physical body now and are looking at it." I paused. "Now describe to me what you see."

"I see the body of a black woman. She has a very sore back as well as sore shoulders and arms. She is bleeding a lot. It looks like a very hardened body … a very hard one."

I asked if her body could breathe at that moment. She paused a moment.

"I am dead." She burst into tears.

---

[26] The idea that muscle tension reflects repressed emotions is dominant in body-oriented psychotherapy and is largely associated with Wilhelm Reich.

187

Ana physically struggled for a moment and then kicked and punched aimlessly and in anger. After that she began to relax. A few minutes elapsed before she settled down.

"Observe your body now and tell me what is happening to it," I continued.

"I have passed on. My brothers are taking my body with them. They clean it up and put on my favorite skirt for me. My mother combs my hair, and the others cry and sing hymns in sadness. They put my body on a piece of thick cloth that looks like a canvas and bring me to a place where the black people bury their dead. It is a kind of cemetery."

"What do you feel now?" I asked.

What Ana described next seemed to be consistent with her persistent feelings of anger as her soul consciousness left her body.

"I am very angry. I am going out madly in search of my aggressor. I am trying to retaliate and harm him physically but somehow I cannot; it seems unachievable. Then I decide to harass him mentally and make him go crazy."

"How do you make him go crazy?"

"I attach myself to his thoughts, day and night. I'm like a shadow to them. He will remember my bloody figure and hear my whines repeatedly."

Ana's description was consistent with that of a thought form, the nature of which has been explained in an earlier chapter. In essence, it is a non-physical entity that has been created from thought in the mental and astral plane of the target individual.

"I am getting back at each and every one of those who tortured me, until they feel the torment of the pain that I suffered from each and every lash they inflicted on me."

These statements sounded heavy to me. In an era where slavery was rampant and the rule of law was weak, revenge provided a way to maintain order. Yet, it came with a price. Instead of helping one to move on, it kept the individual dwelling on the situation. I decided to direct her to fast-forward the story of her past life.

"Move on and tell me what happened eventually."

"The tall, white man who is in his sixties, and is the lord of the mill, is turning crazy at the images of my bloody body in his mind. Over time, he is unable to take it anymore. He finally holds up a gun, points it to his head ... and fires! The fatal bullet goes through his skull from one side to the other. I see him falling to the ground, with tremors throughout the body."

At this point a smile of satisfaction appeared on Ana's face. She seemed to feel contented with the outcome of her pursuit. "I can finally rest now," she said.

"What are you experiencing now?"

"Darkness," she said. "This place where I am in now seems to be part of a spiritual realm. It is very dark and full of dead bodies. I am feeling a lot of pain. I am wandering here and unable to find the exit."

I asked her to fast-forward the scene again to the moment when someone came to rescue her from this place.

"I see a light in the distance approaching me. It is an old man, tall and white, who calmly heads for me." It sounded like her spirit guide, I thought.

"What happens next?"

"He takes me into his arms. I am very tired and am lying unconscious. He takes me away. When I wake up, I'm somewhere else ... in another place that is clear, clean and full of beds. I see myself lying on a stretcher and around me are people who are caring for me."

Ana was very tired, and I ended the session at this point. Thereafter she fell asleep for the next thirty minutes in the couch.

It was an emotionally heavy session. When she subsequently woke up, she had many questions. The mental imagery was new and strange to her and she wondered if the story was a product of her fertile imagination.

I explained that the content of the regression experience had come from her past life memory that resided in her soul consciousness. Her body was reliving the story as if she was inside the slave's body that was being flogged in that lifetime. I added that her healing was incomplete. She needed further therapy sessions to access her deep memory again to desensitize her body to the feelings inflicted by the past life event. This would involve a release of all the residual, trapped tension from her past life.

This explanation gave her the calm and clarity she needed. Her symptoms improved immediately after the session, albeit she was a little exhausted. I gave her another appointment to see me again fifteen days later.

Session 2: Past Life as an Executioner

Ana returned to my office on 4 February. To my pleasant surprise, her pain had almost completely disappeared and everything seemed to be positive. After a review of her progress, I decided to get her back to the same past life to get an assessment of the residual tension.

I allowed Ana to lie down on the reclining couch and relax. Next, I brought her mind through the doorway of her imagination to retrieve the image of the black woman in her previous regression. This turned out to be a very easy task this time.

"She is here," Ana began, "... but she is quieter than before, and has recovered."

I then asked Ana to establish a dialogue with her past life self and observe what sensations and feelings that life would load onto her body. The purpose was to get her body to bring out the story and resolve the issue through psychodrama and somatic release.

"Anger and pain," she responded promptly. "It's the physical pain from the lashes, and the anger against my steward."

"Ask your slave woman self if there are still some outstanding issues she needs to resolve."

"The answer is yes. She said that she doesn't understand why there is so much suffering and pain in her life."

On hearing her response, I decided that Ana was ready to experience another past life regression. With her remaining on the couch, I guided her to go through a breathing exercise while concentrating on her breath. Then I directed her attention to the back of her body.

"Focus on your back, Ana."

"It is hurting a lot."

"Concentrate on the pain. I'm going to count backwards from ten to one, and when I'm done you will go back to a lifetime that is associated with this pain. Ten, nine, eight ..." I started counting slowly. When I reached the count of one, I asked, "Now, where are you?"

"I'm in a farm." Ana had just regressed to another past life. "I'm not alone. I am a male in this lifetime, a tall, white man in my forties with graying hair."

"Describe your clothing to me."

"I am wearing a white shirt with the sleeves rolled up to the elbow and a pair of high leather boots, with dark pants inside the boots. I have a slender whip in my right hand."

"Describe the environment you are in."

"Not sure if it's morning or early evening. There is a river nearby and I hear the sound of horses and screams."

"How do you feel now?"

"Excited and anxious. I've found him, finally."

"Whom have you found?"

"I travel along the river border and follow the direction taken by my men. I'm going to the sugar cane field and now I am stopping in front of a young man who is about 1.8 meters tall. He is a slave and appears strong and breathless. I take my whip and lash it on his face. His blood splashes onto my clothes. I tell my men to bring him straight to the torture stake."

It quickly struck me that Ana was now in a role reversal. Such occurrences were frequent in past life regression and generally provided fertile grounds for therapy. From the perspective of the therapist, Ana's chronic pain represented her intrapsychic conflict. As she moved out of her role as victim, to the vantage point of the aggressor, she could now observe her thoughts and behavior in her new role as the executioner, and no longer felt trapped in her own defenses as the victim.

"What happened next?" I asked.

"I see him being tied up. Then I command my men to bring the other slaves over and ..." Ana hesitated and paused.

The story came to a standstill. Then Ana suddenly burst out in tears and cried, "My God, what have I done!"

It seemed that Ana had just developed an insight with regards to the chronicity of her body pains. She continued to cry convulsively.

"What happened?" I asked.

With a trembling voice Ana replied that her past life self had beaten the young man to death, and she couldn't accept the extent of violence inflicted on that slave.

"What did he do to deserve all that?"

"It's only because he disobeyed my orders ... as a white man. I was excited and even angry ... as if that was not enough. I went out to the balcony of the house to light and smoke a cigarette."

"What were your thoughts when you did that?"

"Miserable people … they are mine. I can do whatever I want with them. They're animals, not humans."

Ana's emotional energy seemed to have exploded. Her voice changed and it sounded as if she was a wild beast. She next went into catharsis.

"I did not expect that I would do such a thing." She continued to cry loudly. There was an indication of remorse and I recognized this as an opportune moment to release her tension through asking for forgiveness. I have found that techniques in psychodrama are often useful in such situations.

"Move your body and get on your knees, as if the person you have hurt so deeply is standing in front of you."

While still under trance, Ana moved herself into the kneeling position and said, "Forgive me," repeating the apology several times. The emotional energy continued to remain strong for a long while.

I next gave Ana a pillow which she embraced for a long time. Then I asked her, "Who are you hugging?"

"The young man whom I hurt; he's here."

I waited for a moment before I asked her to release the pillow. What she said next seemed to indicate that healing had begun.

"I'm back next to that torture stake. We are seated and looking at each other."

Ana had stepped out of the scene now and appeared relaxed. I asked her what it was like to get in touch with her inner self again.

"I have reconnected with my past. That event explains why I have been suffering this pain for so long. I am surprised to find myself in the role of the executioner. What I have experienced here will continue to guide me on my spiritual path and never will

I make this mistake again. I understand that anger and hate does not help at all."

It was a profound statement and I stayed in respectful silence.

"This is the biggest lesson of my life ... not to mistreat my physical body." Her voice was softening.

"How do you feel now?" I asked.

"Peaceful."

"Stay with that experience, and let peace be in your mind. Staying in peace and tranquility is the cure for your pain."

Next, I asked Ana to visualize the imagery of a healing garden, and stay there to take advantage of the lovely place to meditate and gain greater awareness of herself. I then left her in the meditative state for a few minutes before I spoke to her again.

"How do you feel now?"

"Well ... painless and quiet."

Ana emerged from her trance state with a smile. I arranged to follow up with her in thirty days' time. We marked our calendars and she left with a most beautiful and impressive smile.

Deep healing had started.

Session 3: Release of Residual Anger

A month later, Ana returned punctually for her appointment. To my pleasant surprise, there was a further improvement in her physical symptoms. Furthermore, she had maintained the same smile on her face since the last time she had left my clinic.

The dosage of her medication had been significantly reduced. She had been taken off her mood stabilizers and analgesics, and was in the process of weaning off her antidepressants. I asked her if the pain was still there. She replied yes, but with a much lesser intensity.

Her reply intrigued me. I wondered why she wasn't totally pain-free during this thirty-day interval, and intuitively I sensed that her healing might be incomplete.

After I got her to relax on the couch, I said, "I want you to close your eyes and think about what has been making you angry in your daily life. Then go back to a situation where you feel you have overreacted. Think about what was said to you, the voice tone that was used, the look of the person saying it and the fairness of the situation. (pause) While you are doing so, let your subconscious mind retrieve the memory. Experience the feelings inside you and make them stronger. Now locate these feelings in your body ... Where are they?"

"In my back and shoulders."

The presence of an associated physical location made the processing of an emotion much easier in hypnotherapy. I decided to help her to embody the emotion with some physical attributes to facilitate the process.

"Describe how you feel."

"I feel a rising energy that is moving incessantly. It is anger."

"Can you give a color to your anger?"

"Yes, it's dark gray."

"Give it a shape."

"It's like a rock."

With these attributes, I formulated a guided imagery script. "Focus on the dark gray rock that represents your anger. Feel the energy moving through your chest to the shoulder, down the arm past the elbow and forearm, and all the way to the wrist and hand. Feel it ... feel the texture, color and movements of this emotion. It's so bad that you just want to get rid of it. (pause) The next thing you do is to open your fingers, make it explode out of your hand and release it. You have no place for this bad feeling. You can feel yourself screaming. Let it out now. Imagine that the scream will dissipate and disintegrate, and you will begin to feel relieved."

I paused for a moment and resumed.

"Now, you are feeling calm and happy to be rid of the unpleasant sensation. A few moments ago, you had all the emotion inside you, and now it's gone. What remains now is a wonderful feeling of calm and peace within you. With all this comes the peace of mind and clarity of thought and vision. In future, when you experience emotions like anger, you will be able to release it rapidly. You are learning to be a more relaxed person."

As Ana was coming out of her hypnotic state, she looked refreshed and rejuvenated. Several things came to light in the course of this session. She had since completely understood the reason for all the pain and suffering she had been experiencing.

I noticed further improvement in Ana shortly after she completed her therapy. She was very happy because she could now stop reacting to her feelings of anger, and she could keep everything under control without the need for medication.

As she was leaving my clinic, I reassured her that everything would be fine and I would review her six months later.

Follow-up

Ana came back for one more appointment to my office on 22 October. It was a moment of joy when I found her completely pain-free this time! In retrospect, I had managed to uncover enough of her past for her to find explanations for the pain she felt. I had also managed to help her stop her bodily responses to the anger that she had experienced in some of her current life situations. This phenomenon could happen only when her current body became aware that the previous life was over after reliving the past life story.

In general, the attempt to make patients recall traumatic events from their past lives eventually leads the individuals to resolve their current life symptoms, even though the trauma resides in a different lifetime, a different culture and a different historical era. The idea behind past life therapy is that the traumatic events impact on the psyche and the physical body to generate a memory record. The memory record remains frozen after the death of the body and is carried over by the soul consciousness to a different life, where it continues to cause impressions that shape the personality. This can generate various types of illnesses. By facilitating the patient to relive these situations, the emotional and physical burdens can be released while the meaning underlying those burdens is reframed.

As therapists, our goal is to lead our patients to integrate their past memories into the totality of their personal awareness. Unless the dissociated elements of the trauma are integrated completely into their personal consciousness, there will be repercussions on the current personality.

Much of my effort was spent on cleaning up Ana's anger and psychological noise that prevented her from harmonizing with her life. Doing so had helped her to find a way to understand the real cause of her illness and allow healing to take place. With an understanding of the meaning of the illness in her life, she was able to take the healing process on to a transformational level. This was part of a "deep memory processing" that promoted self-knowledge and changes in her behavior.

CHAPTER EIGHT

Metaphor for Autoimmune Disorder

Dr. Natwar Sharma

"The natural healing force within each of us is the greatest force in getting well."

Hippocrates

Regression therapy first caught my attention about five years ago. After graduating from medical school I specialized in Pediatrics and thereafter trained as a pediatric intensivist. I went on to complete MRCPCH from London, UK, after which I was feeling contented, as if there was little more to be done in life.

Initially, when I evaluated various and complementary healing practices, my judgment was clouded with doubt and disbelief. Over time, my prejudice gave way to a spirit of inquiry and I owed this change in attitude to my spiritual guru who taught me meditation. Instead of rejecting non-conventional treatment blindly, I became increasingly more open to consider the ideas and the multiple possibilities offered by these alternative healing modalities. I started to broaden my perspective of therapeutics by looking at various alternative therapies and in the process I became involved in learning regression therapy.

My Journey as Therapist

My first patient in regression therapy turned out to be a fellow medical colleague in Pediatrics. He was a close friend of mine who had a problem of chronic depression and chronic fatigue syndrome.[27] While he initially doubted the effectiveness of the treatment, a part of him was curious to understand how the modality worked. He had been suffering from chronic depression and felt stuck in his life. For years, he had been consuming multiple antidepressants with hardly any discernible benefit. After going through the therapy with me, he experienced a dramatic, positive response and we were both astonished. Two sessions of regression therapy were all that was needed for him to rid himself of his psychological ailment. He had since stopped taking all medication and was now enjoying a marked improvement in his quality of life.

Soon afterwards, another unique experience changed my worldview. It involved a lady patient who had aplastic anemia. While the regression therapy process appeared straightforward in her case, the insights derived from her past life story changed my entire outlook. This incident also marked a turning point in my career.

During the therapy session, the patient regressed back to a past life in which she happily grew up in a rich family and was married to a wealthy landlord in India. Her life continued to remain happy after she gave birth to a son whom she expected to be her eventual heir. Unfortunately her son, after growing up, turned out to be an utter disappointment. He was addicted to both alcohol and gambling, and in addition ill-treated the mother. As

---

[27] Chronic fatigue syndrome is a group of debilitating medical conditions characterised by persistent fatigue that is unrelated to exertion, unrelieved by rest and not caused by other medical conditions.

the story unfolded, she eventually became a widow, and at the age of seventy when she should have been expecting her son to be a source of support, protection and security, a disaster occurred. Her son assaulted her when she refused to transfer her property to his name. He hit her on the head with a flower vase and took her life.

Reviewing this past life in the light of her problem of an autoimmune aplastic anemia, it suddenly dawned on both the patient and myself that the story offered a metaphoric narrative that was being played out as a thematic parallel to her medical illness.

Aplastic anemia is a rare blood disorder in which the stem cells, or mother cells, residing in the bone marrow are damaged. As a result, these mother cells fail to manufacture all the three types of daughter cells, the red blood cells (RBCs) and white blood cells (WBCs) and platelets for the blood circulation. The damage to the stem cells may be caused by exposure to a variety of agents including chemicals, drugs, radiation, infection and heredity. In the autoimmune variety of the disease, it is known that the patient's WBCs attack their own stem cells and cause the bone marrow production to fail.

In this patient, the metaphoric imagery of the son's fatal attack on the mother provided not only a physical parallel but also a basis to the metaphysical meaning of her aplastic anemia. At the same time, the symbolic interpretation provided her with the motivation for self-healing. From the metaphorical perspective, the son was represented by the WBCs that were normally a part of the body's immune system, which was supposed to play a protective role. The stem cells, on the other hand, represented the mother. In the development of an autoimmune disease, the patient's immune system had turned aggressive against her own body cells and tissues. In this case, the patient's WBC attacked her own body stem cells fatally to give rise to aplastic anemia.

Stories are well known for their power to enrich our lives and shape the way we view and interact with the world. Past life stories, in particular, reveal the wonders of the human spirit and play a creative role in helping patients develop their innate skills to cope with difficult life situations. Metaphorical narratives, being embodiments of experience, play an important role in the healing process especially when healing takes place through communication with the use of a patient-generated metaphor. The symbolic organization that represents the mind-body system that produced the metaphor reveals meaningful information to the patient for healing to occur. Upon acquisition of this insight, the patient's requirements for blood transfusions reduced dramatically. Her hemoglobin level also stabilized. My perception of healing has never been the same since.

Autoimmune diseases are frequently encountered in my practice. In the following section, I am sharing in detail the outcome of regression therapy of another patient with an autoimmune disease. She had systemic lupus erythematosus (SLE), an autoimmune disease that can affect the connective tissues of any part of the body. Like in other autoimmune disorders, the immune system attacks the patient's cells and tissues, resulting in chronic inflammation and tissue damage. In this case, the patient benefited from a similar metaphoric intervention during the regression process.

THE CASE OF AISHWARYA – SYSTEMIC LUPUS ERYTHEMATOSUS

Aishwarya was a thirty-eight-year-old, middle-class working woman who had been suffering from SLE for the past one year.

Her doctors had taken a long time to diagnose her disease, and she was unhappy with the short-term relief that she obtained with their prescribed medication.

The cause of SLE is unknown. Like in all autoimmune disorders, the patient's immune system starts to attack the body's own healthy tissues. As a rule, the most common tissues involved are skin, joints, heart, lungs, blood vessels, liver, kidneys and nervous system. The course of the disease is unpredictable and characterized by flares and remissions. The illness itself presents with a variety of symptoms, the most common being a skin rash on the cheeks, fever, malaise, joint pains, muscle pains, fatigue and temporary loss of cognitive abilities.

In Aishwarya's case, her predominant disease symptom was that of joint pains. She had been told that there was currently no cure for SLE and that the current medical treatment approach used medication to suppress her own body's immunity.

As Aishwarya stepped into my consultation room, she impressed me as a shy, reserved, traditional Indian woman. Clothed in a simple outfit, she showed a sad and depressed countenance. Her activities and movements were notably slow for her age, and her voice was meek. She had separated from her husband a couple of years ago and had since been taking care of her two teenage daughters single-handedly. Working as a government employee, her work had been adversely affected since the onset of her sickness.

As I probed into her clinical history, she revealed that she had lately been experiencing persistent generalized body aches and joint pains throughout the day. The pains were affecting her shoulders, elbows, knees and ankles. This was associated with fatigability and severe lethargy and limited her work capacity. She had also experienced chest pain with breathing difficulty for the past six months. This was associated with tingling and numbness all over the body whenever she remained still. As a result, her ability to concentrate had diminished. She also added that, whenever people around spoke loudly, it would startle her and cause palpitations. Sleepless nights had become common since the onset of her illness. She felt sad and helpless and brooded a lot as to why she was afflicted with the illness.

After three months of doctor hopping and extensive laboratory investigations, she was eventually diagnosed to have SLE. Her laboratory report revealed elevated levels of inflammatory markers and anti-nuclear antibodies. She was currently under the care of a rheumatologist. As her condition was a complicated one, I was reluctant to take on her case, but I realized she had come with high hopes. One of her colleagues had experienced a positive outcome of her sickness with regression therapy and had recommended the treatment strongly to her. After some hesitation, I agreed to treat her, but only on the condition that she continued with her regular medications from her rheumatologist. To that she agreed.

I next probed into her social, marital, family and emotional history. Her husband was psychotic and had delusions of infidelity. He had abused her physically and verbally and she had since separated from him. She continued to experience immense hatred for him, and had been spending a lot of her time brooding over her past misfortune. She felt very insecure and was concerned over the future of her daughters.

"What do you think you need most at the moment?" I enquired, as I was elucidating her clinical history.

"Love," she answered unhesitatingly.

I was impressed.

Aishwarya had taken good care of her husband and did everything she could for him. Yet he had never cared to make her happy. She felt fine that he was not around physically to trouble her, but continued to brood over why she'd had to suffer because of him.

Past Life as Chameli

Aishwarya turned up for her first formal therapy session on 4 December 2012. Relaxed on a couch, she went through the hypnotic induction phase smoothly. As she was entering the trance state, a thought surfaced spontaneously.

"My body pains make me feel sad and helpless," she said.

This statement struck me as being emotion-laden. I immediately decided to leverage on it and instructed her to repeat this statement several times slowly to vivify her associated feeling. Next, I told her to focus on the word "helplessness" as a reference to the feeling. Using this reference, I slowly guided her subconscious mind to regress back to the first point in time when this feeling was felt. This maneuver, which is commonly known to therapists as the "affect bridge" technique, immediately connected Aishwarya with a past life situation in which her subconscious mind had previously experienced the anxiety of being helpless.

"I am a young girl, by the name of Chameli," she began. "I am growing up in a middle-class family with loving parents, one brother and one sister. I am experiencing a lot of joy and happiness in that simple family."

The story was gathering momentum and I allowed her to talk freely.

"It is daytime in a hilly area. I am a nineteen-year-old girl and riding on the carriage of a tractor. I am feeling happy in the company of my friend and several other young teenage children are around me."

"Which country are you in?"

"It is North India, in a place called Kulu."

Kulu is the capital of the Kullu District, in the Indian state of Himachal Pradesh. Kullu is a broad open valley formed by the Beas River, and is famous for its beauty and its majestic hills covered by pine and deodar forests.

"Describe your clothing and footwear to me."

"I am wearing a churidar[28] and rubber slippers on my feet."

"Tell me what is going on."

"There are ten of us in a carriage. We have finished harvesting the rice field and are on our way home, sitting on top of the rice bags in the carriage."

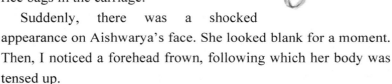

Suddenly, there was a shocked appearance on Aishwarya's face. She looked blank for a moment. Then, I noticed a forehead frown, following which her body was tensed up.

"What happened?" I asked.

"While turning on the Ghat road[29], the carriage jerked because one of its wheels went over a stone. That caused my friend to fall off from the carriage and accidentally roll down into the deep valley."

Tears rolled down her cheeks as she was describing the scene. She could not control herself anymore and a sob escaped from her throat. Following that she cried bitterly.

"I am frozen with fear. The sight is so pathetic and shocking. I am feeling very sad. My friend is badly hurt. Her hair is matted with blood. She is a beautiful girl and nobody is able to help her. I am helpless, and can't do anything about it. We can only watch

---

[28] Churidar is a traditional Indian dress consisting of tight-fitting trousers that are cut widely at the top and narrow at the ankle. They are sometimes also referred to as a Punjabi costume.

[29] Ghat roads are the name of the access routes into the mountain ranges of the Indian Subcontinent and are built to connect to the Hill Stations. Most of them contain a number of sharp hair-pin bends.

the disaster."

"What is preventing you from helping her?"

"It is not possible to get down the valley to rescue her. It is too deep down and there is no road access." She covered her face with her hands and cried. She was in full catharsis.

"She is only twenty years old and is my good friend. She was just beside me a moment ago before she fell, and now I can't do anything to save her. I feel very guilty. No one is able to reach her."

After Aishwarya stopped crying, I instructed her to move on to the next significant event of this past life.

"I am now a young woman of twenty-one years of age, fair and good-looking. I am wearing a red sari and newly married to a man in a middle-class family. The house that we are staying in is in the same hilly area. I am feeling suffocated and unhappy.

"What's the reason for this feeling?"

"My husband has a very suspicious personality. He doesn't allow me to go out of the house alone. He won't even tolerate any man talking to me. His parents (my in-laws) are similarly suspicious. I feel sad and lonely and miss my parents. I am socially restricted but have no choice but to comply, because it is against the cultural tradition to question the husband or in-laws. My parents have paid dowry to get me married. My in-laws rarely speak politely. Instead they are always yelling at me. I spend my nights silently crying. On top of that, my husband doesn't support me."

What Aishwarya described was a typical Indian cultural tradition. In most parts of India, many women have to put up with similar behavioral and social restrictions. They have to cover their faces with a veil, and restrict their activities to only household work. They are not supposed to confront their elders, including their parent-in-laws. In recent decades, however, the situation has improved and women in general are more liberal.

"A young man from our neighborhood is visiting us," she continued. "Oh dear ...!" she suddenly exclaimed.

There was a pause and I sensed fear in her tone.

"He is praising my beauty in front of my whole family!" With a trembling voice she continued, "He says that I am one of the most beautiful women he has ever seen, and he would pray to God to have a wife like me."

I sensed trouble brewing in the story.

"As he is speaking, I am feeling very scared because I am anticipating some adverse consequences," she said with a sigh. "True enough, after the young man left, my husband and his parents start yelling at me."

There was a sad countenance on Aishwarya's face. I also noticed that she was beginning to clench her fists.

"I am feeling dizzy, and body pains are worsening." There was a change in tone. I noticed that she had turned restless and was squirming in the therapy chair.

After a brief pause, I asked, "What happens next?"

"That same night, my husband and parent-in-laws corner me and lock me in my room. I feel like a helpless deer surrounded by the three of them. I feel panicky and my heart is pounding. My husband is tying a cloth over my mouth. He is picking up a stick and is beating me until my body is becoming bruised. I am covering up my face in pain and fear." As she said so she arched up her body into a crouching position and covered her face with both hands.

"My parent-in-laws are tying up my hands behind me. They are blaming me for having an affair with the neighbor boy. They are kicking me. I am unable to cover my face now that my hands are tied, and my face is receiving blows from their kicks." Tears were rolling down as she sobbed. This progressed on to a muffled cry.

"I can't move my body now and every part hurts. I feel paralyzed with pain, and I feel like lapsing into an unconscious state."

Aishwarya seemed to be stuck with her story, and I felt the need to prod her on.

"What gives you that feeling?" I asked gently.

"My husband and in-laws are taking away all my jewelry. They are leaving the house now and making the whole incident look like a robbery. I become more conscious intermittently and when I gather more strength I want to get up, because of thirst and hunger. Unfortunately, every little movement gives me terrible pain. I am scared to move."

Aishwarya went into catharsis. Then she continued to describe the agony she went through.

"It takes me a few days to die. My body is filled with pain. I am feeling so hungry and thirsty."

"What are your thoughts at this moment?"

"I am completely fed up. What is the purpose of my existence in this life? My own husband and in-laws, who are supposed to be protecting me, are beating me to death instead. I am being punished for something that is no mistake of mine! It doesn't make sense."

It was an "Aha!" moment. It was as if the clouds in front of me had parted, and the solution to the problem appeared right in front of me. The confusion surrounding the metaphysical origin of SLE suddenly dissolved and the issue was clarified.

Our body's immune system is normally meant to protect us and acts as a defense mechanism against many insults. In Aishwarya's case, her own protective mechanism, as symbolized by her husband and in-laws, had turned aggressive and caused trauma instead of providing protection. Her immune defense mechanism was attacking her own tissues, especially her joints and muscles, to produce antibodies against her own body systems. This cellular memory, which was deeply engraved in her soul consciousness from a past life, was now manifesting in the current life as SLE.

"Death is a relief. I am happy that life has ended," Aishwarya continued.

"What do you conclude about your husband and in-laws?" I asked.

"I will never forgive them for what they have done to me," she said with a sob.

Aishwarya was in deep trance still. However, the purpose of her incarnation into this life of suffering was as yet unclear. After a brief thought, I decided to probe for further clues.

Past life as a European Queen

"Allow yourself to move to another past life that is linked to your current issue at the count of three. One, two and … three."

Aishwarya promptly went to another past life.

"I am a middle-aged woman wearing grand clothes in a big palace. I am the queen."

"Which country are you in?"

"It seems like somewhere in Europe."

"What is happening now?"

"I am always suspicious of my husband, and doubting his character. I am suspecting that three of my maidservants are having an affair with him, the king."

"How does that make you feel?"

"I am furious, and have decided to punish them rigorously. I put them in a dark prison without light and ensure that they starve to death."

"Are they dead now?"

"Yes."

"What are your feelings now?"

"It's a relief, but as time passes by, the truth comes home to me. I realize that they are innocent, and I am feeling guilty about what I have done. I am responsible for the death of three innocent lives, and it is difficult for me to get over it."

There was a pause, after which she started to cry. Puzzled, I asked, "Tell me, what is happening?"

"I just realized that these three maidservants, who were so close to me and who died because of my suspicion, are the same three individuals as my husband and two parent-in-laws who killed me in my past life as Chameli."

This was a significant insight. I mulled it over for a moment and decided to probe further.

"What are your feelings now that you realize their identities?"

"It makes sense to me now! It's like a role reversal."

"Is there an identifiable event in your current life that has the same pattern as your past life as Chameli?"

"There is an incident some three years ago ..." she recalled. "I am at home. It is evening time. My husband is very angry with me. He is questioning my fidelity. I am feeling very sad and upset with his accusation. I argue with him and he responds by hitting me. He is very mean and calls me a prostitute."

Aishwarya was turning emotional.

"The physical pain that he has inflicted on me doesn't hurt as badly as the insult. I feel like ending my life ... but I can't. I have to stay alive for my two daughters' sake. I have been trying to ignore and forget the incident ever since, but it's difficult."

There was a brief pause. I saw the repetitive pattern in her past and present life stories. Her memories of the traumatic events had persisted as unassimilated and fixed ideas that were acting as foci

211

for altered states of consciousness in her various lifetimes. This seemed to be coming back as behavioral re-enactments. I felt it was time that Aishwarya needed to see that pattern for herself.

"Now, pause for a moment and focus on those past life events that have a parallel in your present life," I said.

After a brief pause, I continued, "Put the significant events of your past and present lives together and look at the whole picture that you have constructed."

She frowned for a moment, after which her face muscles relaxed. With a spark of insight she said, "It makes complete sense now." It appeared as if a dark cloud had just cleared from around her face.

"I know what emotions my body has been storing from the past, with all the associated pain and trauma. I need to let go of them."

After Aishwarya emerged from her trance state, she looked a bit dazed. Soon, she gathered herself together and gave a smile. "It feels like I am waking up from a bad and painful dream ... but now I feel fresh and revitalized."

It was a most rewarding therapy session. Aishwarya left my clinic as a changed person.

Concluding Thoughts

My first follow-up appointment with Aishwarya was four weeks later. She said her body pains had reduced by about 80 percent. The symptoms of weakness, numbness, tingling, joint pains, and chest pain with breathing difficulty had completely disappeared.

I reviewed her for a second time two months after that. This time, her body pains had completely vanished. She looked very cheerful, joyful and with a pleasant countenance. She was looking forward to a life free from sadness. In a fascinating manner, she recounted that she had begun to enjoy better sleep and freedom from irritation when people around her spoke loudly. She was also completely relieved of the hatred that she used to feel toward her husband. She was conscious of herself being more magnanimous and forgiving. When her husband had returned home a couple of weeks ago, she remained calm and forbearing. In view of her diminishing symptoms, I suggested that she seek her rheumatologist's advice with regards to adjusting her medication dosages.

When I reviewed Aishwarya for the last time some six months later, she came with her daughters. By then, she was looking happy, jubilant and radiant. She expressed her deep gratitude to me during that visit. Having recently repeated her blood investigations she brought along her laboratory reports to show me that her blood counts had become normal. Her disease-specific autoimmune antibodies (ANA and Anti-Ro) were confirmed negative. Medically, this would mean that her immune system had stopped attacking her own body tissues.

It was a moment of exhilaration, because I had not expected such a dramatic sequence of events.

Aishwarya's rheumatologist had also told her that she was now in remission, and she had stopped taking all her medication for the past two months. It was most delightful news.

I did not manage to follow Aishwarya in the longer term. Otherwise, it would have been interesting to see if her disease remission stayed permanent. After all, there had been reports of SLE getting reactivated even after a decade of being symptom-free.

As I reflected over this case, it dawned on me that metaphors had played a significant therapeutic role. In her case, the basic logic of transformation from illness to wellness had been enacted through culturally salient and metaphorical actions. The metaphoric narrative derived from Aishwarya's past life stories

213

offered a dramatic theme that ran parallel to her medical problem of autoimmunity. The emotion that was associated with the accusation of infidelity had led her close relatives to inflict serious harm on her. This theme had captured both her conscious and unconscious perception, and functioned as a "matching metaphor"[30] to provide the needed symbolism for healing.

In healing, a patient's attention is expected to shift between two domains: her emotion as it affects her and the therapy as an area for her to articulate the emotion. Aishwarya's healing started with a symbolic process, which involved the mapping of her problem onto a story. Along the way the story imbued her illness with a specific meaning. The ability of the metaphor within the narrative to link the sensory, affective and conceptual aspects of her experience allowed her to construct a model of healing transformation that changed the meaning of suffering. The metaphoric connotations yielded new ways of thinking about and experiencing illness. Ultimately, Aishwarya was able to explain her bodily experiences of pain, and appreciate the emotionally charged meanings that gave her suffering its bite. The final and complete release of the cellular memory of trauma had translated into healing at the physiological level.

Acknowledgment

I owe my change in attitude towards alternative, complementary and holistic therapies to my spiritual guru, Shri Parthasarathi Rajagopalachari, who has taught me Raja Yoga meditation.

---

[30] A name introduced by Lankton and Lankton in 1983 for a metaphor in the primary position that offers a dramatic theme parallel to the presenting problem. The matching metaphor is the opening story, the end of which is only told integrally at the end or figured out by the patient's own insight.

CHAPTER NINE

Assisting Reproduction

Dr. Sérgio Werner Baumel

"Being a mother is walking around crying in a smile!
Being a mother is having the world and having nothing!
Being a mother is suffering in a paradise."

Coelho Neto

For most couples undergoing fertility treatment, the ordeal is an emotional roller coaster. It is estimated that, worldwide, 3 to 7 percent of all couples have an unresolved problem of infertility. Approximately one in six American couples and one in seven British couples are currently struggling with infertility. Many of these couples who have undergone treatment will recount how they have lived their lives around the month-to-month cycles of hope and disappointment that revolves around calendar dates of ovulation and menstruation. However, if the cycle of hope and loss is viewed as a life crisis, a role exists for psychotherapy to help them work through their grief, loss, worry and anxiety.

Increasingly, health professionals are concerned with the psychological impact of fertility and prolonged exposure to infertility treatments on mood and wellbeing. Regression therapy is one form of psychotherapy. Given its holistic approach in moving the patient between the mind and the body, it can be used to facilitate the patient to regain a sense of wholeness, security and receptivity that is often lost in the recurring cycles of medical treatment to get the patient pregnant.

Many women feel bad about themselves when they cannot conceive. The stress of non-fulfillment of a wish for a child is often associated with anxiety, depression and even anger. This chapter highlights two cases in which regression therapy seemed to have been useful in a subtle way to help the patient to get pregnant.

THE CASE OF CASSIE NIGHTINGALE – ENDOMETRIOSIS

Cassie Nightingale came to my office one day with an unusual request. She asked to undergo regression therapy, but she showed no signs of distress. A pretty woman in her early thirties, she was well educated and had a beautiful and spontaneous smile. To me, she was genuinely happy and gave me the impression that there was nothing clinically wrong with her. Hence, I was perplexed.

Cassie was a successful lawyer. She was happily married and had a good relationship with her family, friends and colleagues. She loved to sing and go out socially with her husband and friends. She had enough financial resources to live what seemed to be an almost perfect life. In addition, her lifestyle included adequate time for her to relax and de-stress.

What happened was that she and her husband had decided that they had reached a time in their life to start having children. Unfortunately, after trying hard for several months to conceive, she discovered to her dismay that she had endometriosis.

Endometriosis is derived from the word "endometrium", which is the tissue that lines the cavity of the womb. When there is tissue outside the womb that looks like and behaves like endometrium, the illness is termed endometriosis. This endometrial tissue that is located outside the womb also responds to the menstrual cycle, in much the same way as the tissue inside the womb. Hence, at the end of every cycle, when the hormonal changes cause the womb to shed its endometrial lining, the endometrial tissue outside the womb will also break and bleed. However, unlike the menstrual fluid from the womb lining, which is discharged from the body, the blood from this misplaced tissue has nowhere to go. As a result, the tissues surrounding the areas of endometriosis become swollen and inflamed, and form scars over time. This scarring unfortunately reduces the chances of pregnancy.

While Cassie was being started on medication, and undergoing laparoscopic surgery to reduce the bulk of the scarring, her gynecologist informed her that the cause of this disease was unknown. However, it was highlighted to her that psychosomatic factors were contributory in its etiology.

Being of a happy and cheerful disposition, Cassie could not identify any apparent psychological problem in her current life. As such, she rationalized that any psychological root could only be found in other lifetimes. Hence she came to me for help.

At the outset, I could not ensure her that past life regression therapy would help her condition. Nonetheless, after our initial discussion, we concluded that the option could be worth trying. We settled for a short course of weekly therapy, and it was on condition that she agreed to continue with her ongoing gynecological treatment.

Session 1: A Good Witch in Past Life
On her first therapy session, Cassie went easily into a deep trance state after an initial induction. She readily entered into a

regression experience and saw herself as a woman in her early forties. Gradually, she visualized herself being locked in some kind of dungeon, but was unable to make out any further details. I chose not to press her to develop that scene, and instead brought her further back in time.

At the next scene, Cassie saw herself living in a cottage in the woods. She was talking to a young blonde lady who was asking for her help. The lady wanted an abortion, but Cassie did not want to do it. However, the young lady was desperate. Apparently, she was the daughter of somebody important in the village, and was not supposed to have become pregnant. As she could not afford her gravid state to be discovered and made known, she needed to terminate her pregnancy badly. In the end, Cassie agreed to help.

Next, Cassie went to the woods to hunt for and collect the

necessary herbs. She saw herself carefully picking the right herbs and returning to her cottage. After that, she cleaned the herbs and made them into a potion, which was something like a soup.

She gave some of the potion to the blonde girl and instructed her to rest. The potion caused the womb to contract, but unfortunately something went seriously wrong. The girl started to experience excessive bleeding, so much so that Cassie had to call for help. Help came and the girl was whisked away.

Shortly afterwards, she was arrested by the authorities and taken to the dungeon. At this point, Cassie recognized that it was the same dungeon within which she was locked in the initial scene.

Following the incident, Cassie was accused of being a witch. After some time she was taken away to be publicly executed.

After spending so many days in the dungeon with hardly any food she was physically weak. She could not fight back when people started kicking her. Eventually she was taken to a scaffold, waiting to be hung. However, she was so weak that she could not even stand. Hence they decided to execute her in a different way. They tied her to a horse that was then made to run, dragging her along until she died.

Although this past life story involved a pregnancy, the spiritual lesson for Cassie was not immediately clear. I encouraged her to reflect over the story from a broader perspective. At first, she thought the lesson was that she should wisely exercise her choice with regards to whom she should help. Soon, she recognized that the more likely lesson was that she must not choose. Rather, she should help whoever it was within her ability to help. Also, she must not blame herself for other people's mistakes. Following that, she received a message from her Higher Self saying, "I hope that now you have learned."

Over the following week, Cassie searched the Internet for medicinal herbs. Among the herbs she saw herself collecting, two of them were found to be contraindicated for pregnant women: the sage (*Salvia officinalis*), which can cause uterine contractions, and the milfoil (*Achillea millefolium*), which can cause uterine bleeding.

Session 2: Past Life Clara – Abuse and Sorrow

Cassie came for her next therapy session a week later, and the theme of the second past life story was also related to pregnancy. However, it was a tragic story. Cassie saw herself as a young nun whose name was Clara. She was sexually abused by a priest, whom she recognized as being her father in her present lifetime, and eventually became pregnant. The head nun came to know of the incident and tried to compel her into having an abortion.

However, Clara managed to escape from the nunnery and ran to a small village.

There in the village, she gave birth. However, one of the midwives who helped her in her delivery took the child away. Heartbroken, she subsequently returned to the nunnery where she stayed for the rest of her life, always feeling guilty for letting her child be taken away.

As we were integrating this experience together, she realized that the lesson she distilled from this story was that she should not leave her goals unattained. Rather, she must keep fighting for what she believed in. It was important for her to make a stand and defend her ideals, and dare to live the life she wanted.

Session 3: Past Life José Manuel – Rejection and Anger

As a surprise, the regression theme took on quite a different slant during the third therapy session.

Cassie saw herself as a young boy in Portugal, in the eighteenth or nineteenth century. The boy's name was José Manuel Alcântara da Silva, son of Pedro Luiz Alcântara da Silva. He grew up in a very rich family but received very little attention from his mother. He resented her indifference and, over time, became angry and aggressive in his temperament. In one of his temper tantrums, he accidentally fell from his bedroom window from the second floor of his house and became paraplegic.

After some time, his mother gave birth to another baby boy. Soon, José Manuel felt very jealous of his younger brother, and tried to kill the baby by suffocation. Fortunately, this was discovered and he was stopped in time. The baby's life was saved, but life took on a different turn for him.

After this incident, José Manuel was sent to a Catholic seminary, where he studied with other boys of his age. He was discriminated against and rejected by the other boys because of his physical disability. He was being bullied, and as his anger escalated, he developed frequent outbursts of aggressiveness. As a result, he was punished and eventually labeled as being possessed by a demon.

This situation continued until it became intolerable. One day he tried to take his own life by cutting his wrists. He lost a lot of blood and became very weak, but did not die immediately. He became moribund, contracted pneumonia and ultimately died from it.

After transiting through the death point, José Manuel continued to wander around his parents' house as a soul. Witnessing the subsequent birth of a younger sister, Cassie recognized this girl as being her mother in the present lifetime. After some years in this situation, José Manuel was led through a "tunnel of light" to "the other side" by a spirit guide. Interestingly, he could sense that this guide was his grandfather.

After Cassie emerged from trance, we both agreed that there was little in the story content that was related to her problem of infertility. However, Cassie did receive from her Higher Mind a message, saying that "each of us expresses our love in his or her own way" and that "we should not keep our feelings to ourselves, but rather tell each other what we feel."

As the message remained unclear in terms of relevance to her infertility, we decided to work through another regression session together.

Session 4: Abortion
On her fourth regression, Cassie saw herself as a young Spanish girl, whose father owned a piece of land and raised sheep. She fell in love with a young shepherd lad named Marcos.

Her father disapproved of her romantic relationship with the shepherd lad and forbade them to continue dating. At first, she was able to restrain herself and keep herself away, but after a while she changed her mind and they decided to run away together. Unfortunately, they did not manage to go far. Her brother went after them, and brought her back while letting Marcos escape.

She was locked inside the house as a punishment. Later, she was forced by her family to date an older man, whom she described as "disgusting". The subsequent story was tragic. The man raped her, but she managed to escape and run away again. She eventually found Marcos and sought shelter with his parents. Soon afterwards, she discovered that she was pregnant from the disgusting old man.

Marcos' mother helped her to obtain an abortion. Unfortunately, after the procedure she could no longer conceive. Despite the setback, she married Marcos, and after some years they adopted a baby boy called Júlio. She then lived happily for some years, until she died from a disease that affected her abdomen.

This regression turned out to be a fruitful one. Cassie recognized Marcos as her current life husband. She also recognized the adopted baby as being the same soul as that of the aborted child. Amazingly, this same soul was supposed to come to her as her child in the present life in due course. She received a divine message that this child was destined to arrive soon. In response to this message, Cassie experienced deep emotional changes. After we integrated all these experiences, we were both excited and agreed to suspend the therapy and wait for the medical treatment of her infertility to work.

After the therapy sessions stopped, Cassie did get pregnant, though not right away. Her endometriosis disease receded for a while, but recurred. In addition, she was told by her gynecologist that her husband's sperm motility was "slow". The understanding from that finding was that it would greatly diminish the chances of a successful fertilization. She was then offered artificial reproductive technology as an option. Bearing in mind what she had learned in one of her past life lessons that she should "not leave her goals unfinished", she agreed to go through an *in-vitro* fertilization (IVF). This was a decision she never regretted. The IVF procedure turned out to be a successful one and she managed to carry the pregnancy to full term.

Today, Cassie has a healthy, seven-year-old son, whom she describes as "a fantastic, very clever and very talkative child".

THE CASE OF HANNA THERESA
– THE INCIDENTAL PATIENT

Hanna was a fellow colleague of mine, and an excellent physician with an interest in regression therapy. She had no problems accepting the concept of reincarnation as it aligned with her religious belief system in Spiritism. She had been participating in a study group in regression therapy that we had run for some months, and within this group a strange incident happened one day.

Hanna was a very loving woman, always considerate in her behavior towards other people, making her best effort to be righteous and helpful to others without hurting anyone. She was in her early thirties and had been married for a couple of years. At one stage after joining our study group, she was seriously thinking of becoming pregnant.

She had often manifested doubts about her ability to raise children and be a good mother. This was strange because she was dealing with children every day in her work, and I noticed that she was very good and loving in her way of handling them. Her relationship with her own parents was also very good and I did

223

not perceive that to be a contributory factor to her fear of motherhood.

Having finally decided she now wanted a child, she stopped contraception and became pregnant shortly afterwards. She was very happy with this. Unfortunately, within less than two months of gestation she started bleeding from her womb, and her pregnancy was in danger. Subsequently an ultrasound imaging showed that there was no viable embryo in her womb, and the pregnancy was naturally interrupted.

Hanna felt very sad with this spontaneous abortion. She started again to suspect that it was because she could not be a good mother. Strangely enough, she was blaming herself for something that seemed to be unreal for all of us who were observing her. She seemed disconnected from whom she was, and this was evident to everyone, except herself. She did not seek therapy; nor did she think a personal change was necessary.

Meanwhile, she continued to participate in our study group. We had been studying different methods of induction in regression therapy all this while. In each meeting, we discussed one particular method, and made out a pair-practice session with one of us being the "patient" and another being the "therapist". This was to test out the method and it also indirectly served as a means of sharing useful regression therapy experience with each other.

By then, it was about three months after Hanna's spontaneous abortion. In one meeting, she volunteered to be the "patient", and I happened to be assigned the "therapist" role.

During the practice session, she went easily into a trance state. As she regressed back in time, she saw herself as a poor woman in the late stages of her pregnancy. She could not identify the time period nor the country in which the past life scene took place, beyond the impression that it was in Europe, either during the Middle Ages or the Renaissance period. She went through an uneventful labor and delivery and gave birth to a boy. However, she was confronted with a disturbing scene in her postpartum period.

"I am walking around in my room," she said. "The baby is crying. He won't stop ... I can't bear this. Why doesn't he stop crying?" Her feelings were one of profound sadness, and she was on the verge of despair.

The sadness worsened as the scene continued. Finally, Hanna saw herself grabbing a pillow and covering the baby's face to muffle the noise, and at the same time suffocated him. The baby died as a result. Hanna became even more desperate, and took her own life.

As she was regressing through the death point, she continued to experience the anguish and the sad, depressed feelings. So I suggested that she go to a quiet, safe place, where she could see all that experience from a higher perspective and obtain healing for herself. From the vantage point of that special place of healing, she calmly analyzed the events she had experienced, and perceived that she was going through a pathological state of postpartum depression.

When she emerged from the trance state, she was impressed by the vividness of the imagery and the profound feelings she experienced. At first, she claimed that she could connect the imagery with her current life issues. We went ahead and discussed as a group of fellow therapists what we had learned from the practice session and finished that meeting, without paying particular attention to her. Little did we realize, however, that Hanna was gradually developing her own insights in the meanwhile, and inner changes were taking place.

About a month after her regression experience, Hanna got pregnant again. I was pleasantly surprised and felt happy for her.

This time the pregnancy went well. Strangely enough, her fears in her ability to become a good mother had vanished. After nine months of gestation she gave birth to a healthy baby boy. Her son is now twelve years old, and she has been a loving and caring mother, just as all of us who knew her well had expected.

Concluding Thoughts

The role of regression therapy in assisting reproduction remains unclear, and no direct cause-and-effect is claimed in these two cases. However, its use in such situations has highlighted the multi-layered psychology of a complex human experience that we regard as a problem of infertility.

The two cases described here differed in their reproductive issues. Artificial methods of reproduction are known to encourage a split between the mind and the body, because the female body now becomes the object of medical scrutiny while the woman's mind and its emotions become neglected and isolated in anxiety. Presumably, this is an area where regression therapy may have a role in restoring some form of mind-body balance.

In Cassie's case, her husband had low sperm motility and her endometriosis further lowered the chance of conceiving. While the use of IVF had taken the uncertainty of fertilization out of her concern, she still needed the mental and emotional wellbeing to provide a nurturing environment for the artificially transferred embryo to implant in her womb and reach full term in a healthy state.

In Hanna's case, it was her psychological fear of motherhood that was the obstacle to childbearing. We do not know why she had a spontaneous abortion, but we do know that the preparation of a new identity during pregnancy is a complex task. As the body prepares to accommodate the physical formation of a fetus, the mind undertakes the formation of the mother she might become. The wishes, fears and fantasies of the pregnant woman revolve around questions like: Who is the baby? How will I be as a mother? How will my perceptions about myself change with the pregnancy? What will happen to my relationships with other people following a pregnancy? Expectant mothers seldom think about such issues systematically. More often than not, these issues are worked on subliminally by them, weaving in and out of their dreams and inchoate feelings.

The pregnancy loss in Hanna's case had brought her inner psyche into a nebulous zone between birth and death. It was about her coming to terms with a life that ended just as it was beginning. It was the ripping away of a dream and joy while a senseless emptiness prevailed in its place. Of interest, this theme of "birth and death" seemed to be played out in her regression scene.

In both instances, there seemed to be some feeling of guilt from their past life experiences. In Hanna's case, she might have harbored the belief that her ambivalence about motherhood had led to the pregnancy's demise. She might have felt the guilt that she did not want or deserve the baby enough. Perhaps both Cassie and Hanna needed some self-forgiveness in order to continue with their motherhood journey and, in this respect, through the help of regression.

APPENDIX

Overview of Regression Therapy

Dr. Peter Mack

*"Primum non nocere, 'First, don't make things worse,'
was an essential principle of Hippocrates' medicine.
Nowadays, unfortunately, it seems to have been forgotten.
Conventional modern medicine aims at getting rid of
patients' symptoms. Little, if any, consideration is given to
the fact that some of these symptoms may actually be used
by the body in an attempt to correct deeper disorders.
When this is the case, suppressing the symptom does not
necessarily help the patient."*

Samuel Sagan
In: Regression – Past Life Therapy for
Here and Now Freedom, 1999

What is Regression?

Regression is a process of working with the patient's
subconscious mind to find the root of its nagging psychological
problem and reliving earlier experiences that have caused the
current condition. The process involves the recall of memory, or a
series of memories, of past events while under trance or a "state

of altered consciousness".[31] These forgotten experiences often contain emotional wounds that have remained unhealed and persisted to trigger unexplained thoughts, feelings and semi-conscious convictions that are symptomatic of the current condition. By bringing deeply buried memories to the surface, regression aims to uncover these wounds and obtain clues to resolve the patient's issue, while providing a safe healing environment.

Through working backwards in time, the repressed events of early childhood or infancy are mentally recovered for processing. The facilitating of memory retrieval in such instances is commonly termed "age regression" by hypnotherapists. Over and above the emotion-laden events in one's current life, the underlying cause of the patient's problem can also be found in the memories of traumatic experiences that occurred in other lifetimes. In these situations, the process of memory retrieval is called "past life regression".

Regression as Therapy

Regression therapy is generally conducted under hypnosis or an altered state of consciousness. Following an initial interview and clarification of the presenting symptoms, the patient rests comfortably on a reclining couch and is gently guided through a breathing and relaxation exercise. As the trance deepens, guided imagery and thematic phrases are used to lead the patient into a scene of a past event.

---

[31] An "altered state of consciousness" is an expression used by Arnold M. Ludwig in 1966 in *Archives of General Psychiatry* 15 (3):225. It is brought to common usage by Charles Tart from 1969.

Many techniques besides guided imagery are used for connecting the mind to a previous event or past life event. One approach is to let the patient focus on a recent memory, and encourage him to say whatever comes to mind, as if the situation is being confronted again. Frequently, a feeling that is represented by a thought emerges on its own. The thought is then used as an important lead for identifying the "bridge" that connects with a relevant past event.

Another approach is to have the patient focus on a disturbing sensation in a particular part of the body, and allow the associated imagery and emotion to emerge from that area. As soon as the patient's thoughts, images or emotion intensify with prompting from the therapist, these are followed into a story that emerges in either a past life or an earlier part of the current life. The point of connection with the past is usually the moment at which the patient experienced the emotion during that past event, in the same manner as in the present. This provides the portal into a past life memory, which is frequently a distressing event in our present life that awakens an older memory.

Once embodied in a past life, the patient experiences an identifiable figure, which he feels as another version of him on a myth-like journey in another lifetime. This identifiable figure can be experienced in one of two ways:

(i) He feels the figure as another part of his personality, and yet not quite like himself,

(ii) He feels inexplicably drawn into the strivings and emotional state of this figure, as if he is living in that body.

In whichever case, the past life personality will have a life history of its own, waiting to be unveiled by the regression process.

The reliving of one's past life experience is akin to viewing a fast-forwarded video-recording of one's history in that lifetime. As the story unfolds, the metaphorical significance and archetypal imagery of the events of that lifetime are unraveled by the workings of the subconscious mind. This brings insight as to how his current symptoms could have their origin in that lifetime. Once the patient is brought back to conscious knowledge of his forgotten experience, the symptom often disappears. This is because recognition of his disturbing feeling as belonging to a previous era dissolves the symptomatic projection. He now learns to put his emotion back into its proper time sequence, and healing takes place.

Fig. 4: Healing with Regression Therapy

| PSYCHE | EMOTION | SOMA |

Reframing
Psychodrama
Re-experiencing
Archetypes
Symbolism
Metaphors
Narrative
Past lives

New Meaning

Catharsis

Search for Life Purpose

Physiological Change

Crisis

Hypnotic state

For the believer in reincarnation, he takes the view of the soul as having lived many lifetimes in many other bodies previously, and is now on its learning journey in his body in the current life.

For the individual coming from the "one-life-only" school of thought, he may view the past life phenomenon through the Jungian concept of the "collective unconscious" into which he has dipped, to access the vast collective memory of mankind. While the patient is reliving the past life experience, the therapist may need to assist him to re-enact the past life script in order to unlock and clear the blocked emotions embedded in those disturbing events. Being both a participant and a witness to those events, the patient takes on a new perspective as new meaning emerges. For example, if the patient looks at his suffering in that lifetime from the perspective of the history of evolution of human society rather than the context of his personal issue, it is easier for him to overcome the pain of his personal suffering. This process of apprehending the true nature of the situation is known as "reframing". With each new insight, his attitude towards the past events changes, and this creates a shift in consciousness. This shift may even lead to a change in his character traits as he understands where his emotions are rooted, and why he has been holding on to them. This, in brief, is the basis of transformational healing.

As a patient experiences more past lives, he gathers more strength, and finds it easier to connect himself to a greater life plan and new personal values. As illustrated by the case of Cindy (Chapter 1 and 2), her personal hardships appear less and less overwhelming as she examines her current life plan from both present and past life perspectives. Her struggles become more meaningful as her life purpose becomes more apparent. This stage of the therapy process is characterized by rapid healing.

Mental Imagery

A common question posed by the patient at the end of a fruitful therapy session is: "How much of my regressed experience is real, and how much of it is imagined?" While there is no clear answer to this question, the problem with attributing the basis of mental imagery to imagination is that it begs a bigger question: "Just what is imagination?"

The meaning of imagination is far from clear today. It is a concept that is more frequently invoked than it is analyzed and defined. It has an air of the unscientific about it that often renders it suspect to those people who pride themselves as being rational. In medical school, imagination is often discussed in a psychiatric context, and hence the term is sometimes used interchangeably with delusion, hallucination and fantasy. However, these latter symptoms are not an accurate representation of imagination.

The basic ingredient of imagination is the power to form mental images, and it includes two functions: (i) the capacity to experience mental images, and (ii) the capacity to engage in creative thought. Whenever a person imagines something, his thoughts are undeceived depictions of a world that is not only unreal, but also known to be so. Because he is the originator of these thoughts, he cannot create the illusion of verisimilitude. As soon as that something has been imagined, it has acquired an autonomous ontological status. The imagined world of the individual becomes self-sufficient and does not require the external judgment of another beholder. In other words, the content of the imagined world is true because, *ex hypothesi*, its originator has deemed it to be true.

234

The power of imagination is at the very root of human creativity and spirituality. The vast potential of the mind to create, recreate, transform and heal is only just beginning to be understood. At the empirical level, imagination is the person's inner ability to filter, magnify and modify the visionary data of experience. At the creative level, imagination represents the person's inner ability to transform the raw content of the visionary experience into a work of art. The relationship between mental imagery and imagination remains indistinct, but can be conceptualized as a bridge between perception and thought.

"Working with past life images and allowing them to unfold into scenes and stories is essentially a meditative process. It requires stillness, a certain trust in the creative powers of the deep imagination as well as a readiness to encounter not just appealing but often dark and disturbing images. The abundant evidence from thousands of regression sessions, publications and research shows without doubt that there is a deeper level to what we call our complexes, a layer that has a buried past-life core."

Roger Woolger

The masters of imagination who preceded the psychoanalysts were actually the early poets like Dante, Shakespeare, Blake and Goethe, who explored the vastness of the creative imagination and its healing potential. Freud and Jung followed their exploration by studying dreams and waking visions. Yet today, we seem to encounter difficulty in understanding the very nature of imagination. The obstacle probably lies with the prejudice of academic psychology in its insistence of being self-consciously scientific, in the rigid sense of the word. We continue to be reluctant to adopt the worldview that the right-brain (creative mind) has a way of knowing what is unique unto itself, and need not be controlled by the left-brain (rational mind). At any rate, as regression therapists, our interest is focused on the healing power of regression, rather than on the real-versus-imaginary debate.

Healing in Regression

Hurtful experiences in one's earlier life produce emotional tension. They trigger fear, anger, shame and lack of self-worth. Immature children do not have the strength to integrate these feelings and bring them to resolution because they are often too scary to handle. As a protective mechanism, the mind learns to anesthetize the intensity of the feelings, block off the full conscious experience and leave behind a scar of unprocessed emotional tension. This tension tends to be deeply buried in the inner psyche, but without the individual's conscious awareness.

As the individual disconnects himself from the accumulation of unresolved feelings in his psyche, he no longer believes that the pain of emotions exists. However, the pressure of his unresolved tension can manifest in different ways. The deep-seated anger and hurt feelings distract him from inner peace and rob him of his sense of joy and self-worth. They also weaken his ability to love and distort his values. This unresolved tension can drive him to fulfill distorted needs such as overeating, smoking, drinking alcohol, overworking, or using co-dependent relationships to maintain the anesthesia for the pain. Not infrequently, the repressed emotional tension may spill over and manifest as headache, insomnia, peptic ulcer, irritable bowel syndrome, chronic fatigue syndrome or some other psychosomatic illness.

Healing is a natural, human process and it is about purifying one's heart and regaining wholeness. Regression therapy provides the required setting for that to take place. There is a physiological imperative for our human system to release stress to restore inner balance. That explains the situation where the patient who is undergoing therapy reaches a point that he cannot hold the emotional tension any further, he starts to tear or cry to release the tension. This phenomenon is commonly known as "catharsis", or sometimes known as "abreaction" by hypnotherapists. The trance state makes it much easier for the patient to let go, and this emotional release is needed for healing.

Most of us have been conditioned in our childhood to suppress the release our emotions as part of a social norm. Often, we are afraid to re-experience certain hurtful feelings. Some of our family members have taught us that crying or showing fear or anger is not tolerated, because expressing our emotions is considered a sign of human weakness. The reality is that, when the inner emotions are released in a safe and loving environment reinforced by a patient-therapist rapport, it is a positive and powerful healing mechanism. It cleanses the emotional wounds of the individual, liberates him of the crippling effect and purifies his consciousness. If anything, the tears of catharsis are the very tears that the patient needed to release at the time of the original, hurtful event in childhood, but couldn't because there wasn't a safe environment then. Regression therapy provides the missing structure and allows the process to go into completion. Herein resides the premise for the use of inner child healing in regression. (Chapter 3)

Prenatal Regression

Occasionally, experiences within the womb may also lead to profound influences on the individual's adult life. Prenatal regression can either occur spontaneously or be conducted intentionally by a therapist. The unborn baby is physiologically connected to the mother and psychologically surrounded by her emotional energy. In itself, the intra-uterine fetus lacks emotional defenses and is unable to escape from the impact of the mother's emotional currents.

Our experience with prenatal regression experience indicates that the baby can describe its amniotic-fluid environment and recall intrauterine events at a very early stage of conception. The fetus feels what the mother is feeling, and registers the maternal experiences as its own. It can detect and react to its external environment exactly in the way adults do. As shown by the case of Dana in Chapter 4, the manner in which the fetus adapts to the maternal emotions will define its own emotional pattern and personality development in postnatal life. Hence, a prenatal regression is often used to help a patient sense a mother's psychological state,[32] liberate early negative experiences and uncover the roots of certain unexplained symptoms. As the ego is not yet formed, the fetus cannot distinguish between itself and the extended uterine environment. Hence the emotional state of the

---

[32] "Prescient Human Fetuses Thrive", Sandman, C.A., Davis, E.P., Glynn, L.M. *Psychol Sci*, 2012 Jan 1:23(1)-93-100. Research findings show that the foetus can sense the mother's psychological state and the womb environment is important for postnatal development.

mother is considered to be indistinguishable from that of the fetus.

Historical Perspectives

The idea of reincarnation seems to have its origin in the ancient speculative philosophies of India, although precise dating of the historical sequence of events is difficult to pin down. It is common in Eastern philosophy that people tend to view life as a repetition of eternal cycles and the physical world as illusion, and hence is less concerned with history. However, it is generally believed by experts that the reincarnation concept reached a state of common acceptance around 300 BC.[33]

The concept of hypnosis, on the other hand, existed as early as the fifth century BC when ancient Greeks used sleep temples to cure people of their ailments. However, the decisive moment in its historical development occurred in the 1765 when Franz Mesmer first proposed animal magnetism as a basis and method for hypnosis. Although this was discredited, Dr. Elliotson, the physician who introduced the stethoscope to England, later revived the concept. In 1841, Dr. James Braid developed the eye-fixation method of inducing relaxation and called it "hypnosis". In 1845, Dr. James Esdaile, a surgeon working in India, performed hundreds of minor surgical procedures under hypnotic anesthesia.

In World War One Ernst Simmel, a German psychoanalyst, used hypnosis for the treatment of war neurosis with promising

---

[33] Swami Agehananda Bharati, an Austrian by birth, a leading Western expert on Hinduism and Buddhism, believes that the reincarnation concept came at the time that the Puranas were composed.

results; the soldiers could return to the trenches almost immediately after treatment. During World War Two, hypnosis played a prominent part in the treatment of post-traumatic stress disorder.[34] After World War Two, Milton Erickson had a major impact on the understanding of hypnosis and the mind. In 1955, the British Medical Association accepted hypnosis as a valuable medical tool and in 1958 the American Medical Association recognized hypnosis as a viable scientific modality.

Regression therapy really started to develop in the 1950s when a British psychiatrist, Alexander Cannon, regressed more than a thousand patients with symptoms that were not curable by conventional means, and observed significant improvement. The foundation of regression therapy lies with the concept of making the unconscious mind conscious, and is about restoring choices and healing. By moving backwards chronologically under trance, early childhood memories could be retrieved. Soon therapists realized that they could regress patients not only back to early childhood, but were also able to uncover memories of birth, prenatal and past lives. Hence, it was concluded that an element capable of recording events existed in human consciousness, even in the absence of a physical body.

Denys Kelsey, another British psychiatrist, was an early pioneer of past life regression therapy. He worked with Joan Grant and published their exploratory work on the value of past life therapy in *Many Lifetimes* in 1967. It was in the 1970s that regression therapy really took off. Peter Ramster began his

---

[34]John G. Watkins, "The Psychodynamic Treatment of Combat Neurosis (PTSD) with Hypnosis during World War II", *Int J of Clinical and Experimental Hypnosis*, Vol 48, Issue 3, 2000.

pioneering work in Australia, while Hans TenDam led the way in Europe. In 1978, four further books on past life regression were published: *Reliving Past Lives* by Helen Wambach; *You Have Been Here Before* by Edith Fiore; *Past Lives Therapy* by Morris Netherton; and *Voices from Other Lives* by Thorwald Dethlefsen. These four books had one thing in common, in that they dwell on the symptomatology rather than the spiritual implications of illness.

In the meanwhile, a significant body of evidence on the existence of past lives was being collected by Dr. Ian Stevenson (1918–2007), one of the most prominent research psychiatrists of the twentieth century. He authored around three hundred papers and fourteen books on reincarnation.[35] Instead of relying on hypnosis to verify that an individual had had a previous life, he chose to collect thousands of cases of children who spontaneously remembered their past lives. He documented the child's statements of a previous life and identified the deceased person whom the child remembered being. Then he verified the facts of the deceased person's life that matched the child's memory. He even matched the children's birthmarks and birth defects to the wounds and scars on the deceased persons, as verified by medical records.

Over the next decade, there was a shift in focus and a growing impulse among therapists to look at the existential meaning of life. With this paradigm shift, the Association for Past Life Research and Therapies was founded by fifty therapists in 1980.

---

[35] Dr. Ian Stevenson, "Twenty cases suggestive of reincarnation", in 1966, "European cases of the reincarnation type", in 2003, Reincarnation and Biology: A contribution to the etiology of birthmarks and birth defects" in 1997.

This non-profit organization was dedicated to holding training workshops, and it established criteria of who should practice regression therapy. It published the first *Journal of Regression Therapy* in 1986.

Throughout the 1980s the focus of past life therapy continued to shift towards the concept of the soul's journey. It was becoming clear that where regression therapy supersedes other therapies in terms of effectiveness, it was in the more profound perspective on the meaning of life. Today, the intense concern about whether past life really exists is beginning to wind down, and it is increasing held that reincarnation is more of a philosophy of life than a belief system.

In the 1980s Roger Woolger (1944–2011), a Jungian psychotherapist by background, contributed far-reaching theoretical concepts that helped the regression community to understand past life therapy. He taught his students the value of working with the experience of the body. He also pioneered the technique of combining body psychotherapy with psychodrama to release the traumatic memories embedded in particular body parts.

The First World Congress for Regression Therapy was held in the Netherlands in 2003. In the summer of 2006, the Earth Association of Regression Therapy (EARTh) was founded in Frankfurt. A few years later, Andy Tomlinson, who has been active as a trainer in regression techniques, founded the Spiritual Regression Therapy Association (SRTA) and Norsk forbund for Regresjonsterapi in Scandinavia.

Meanwhile in India, the growth of regression therapy assumed a life of its own. The Life Research Academy was founded in

Hyderabad in 2000 under the leadership of Dr. Newton and Dr. Lakshmi to promote training. In 2010, Dr. Newton launched the Association for Regression and Reincarnation Research (ARRR), a global association to promote research in regression.

As regression therapy gathered momentum, an increasing need to advance the discipline within the field of Medicine was felt. This led to an informal meeting of an international group of physicians and clinical psychologists in Portugal in April 2013. The Society for Medical Advance and Research in Regression Therapy (SMAR-RT) was thus formed with the aim of promoting research into regression.

Indications for Therapy

A wide range of medical disorders are treatable by regression. A physical symptom can be a useful entry point to a past life and acts as a somatic bridge, especially if it is associated with a strong emotion such as fear, anger or guilt. Examples abound. For instance, migraines are often related to negative childhood emotions. Some headaches are connected with intolerable mental challenges while others are related to head injuries in past lives. Some peptic ulcer pains are related to past life experiences of hunger or memories of terror. Neck pains may relate to past life deaths through hanging, strangling or beheading. Even birthmarks are often found to correspond to entry points of penetrating injuries inflicted in past lives.[36]

Irrational fears of all sorts are often, if not almost always, rooted in a past life. They may stem from all kinds of trauma or death from natural disasters in previous lifetimes. For example,

---

[36] "Birthmarks and Birth Defects Corresponding to Wounds on Deceased Person", Dr. Ian Stevenson, *Journal of Scientific Exploration*, Vol 7, No. 4, pp 403-410, 1993.

hydrophobia has been found to be related to drowning, claustrophobia to death from suffocation, acrophobia to death from falling from heights and ophidiophobia to attack by snakes in past lives.

Eating disorders in present life are often re-runs of past life memories of starvation, poverty and famine. Sexual difficulties may reflect underlying past life experience of sexual abuse and rape. Unexplainable guilt sometime stems from past life memories of having directly killed loved ones, or from feeling responsible for the death of others. Depression can also sometimes be related to past life memories of unfinished grieving for the loss of a loved one, or despair from war and starvation. Unexplainable feelings of insecurity may be caused by past life memories of separation, abandonment or being orphaned.

Beyond physical disorders, regression therapy is effective in many emotional and behavioral disorders. This includes relationship problems, low self-esteem, loss of self-love, low self-worth or a struggle to find one's life purpose, as illustrated by the case studies in this book.

Unsuitable Subjects

Occasionally, hypnotic regression does not produce the desired results in some patients. If there is difficulty getting into a sufficiently deep trance, the patient may not get into a past life, or if he does, he is unable to fix on it. In such cases, the patient may experience a series of unrelated images from various lives, with a mix of people from changing eras that come and go. Such images are often meaningless. At other times, factors that contribute to the failure may include:

(i)   The patient may lack the emotional strength to integrate the insights from the therapy.

(ii)   The patient may have deep anger arising from early childhood trauma that blocks the process.

(iii)   The patient may be afraid of exposing himself and unconsciously blocks attempts at self-revelation.

(iv)   The patient's belief system conflicts with the concept of reincarnation, and unconsciously resists a past life entry.

(v)   The patient is not prepared to take ownership of his own healing because he feels that he has a predetermined destiny to suffer.

(vi)   The patient has a mental hurry or expectation of a rapid or miraculous change.

(vii)   The patient holds on to his symptoms and is unwilling to give them up because of secondary gains, especially if he fears that a loss of his "special" position after the therapy may deny him the due attention from his loved ones.

Regression for Medical illness

In the second half of the last century, advances in medical knowledge and technology have shifted our understanding of human illness almost completely to a biomedical framework. Since then, the distinction between "illness" and "disease" has largely been lost.

Illness is what a patient experiences while disease is what the medical practitioner diagnoses on the basis of the presenting symptoms, clinical signs, laboratory investigations and radiological imaging. Science has accumulated a large knowledge base of facts that can explain with increasing reliability how the human individual operates as a biological organism. Yet, it can say very little of relevance for the deep caves of a person's specific life, or the essence of his being. Science can describe the patient's physiology through quantitative measurements of bodily functions such as blood pressure, respiration, temperature, pulse oximetry, urine output, hematology, blood biochemistry, serology, ECG and EEG waveforms, and weave them into a scientific story. However, these physiological descriptors tell nothing about the patient's experience of his own body and the state of his being.

What then is "being"?

"Being" is the patient's discovery of the deepest knowledge of himself and of the purpose of his existence, through understanding the plain and simple moments of his everyday life. It is the discovery of his capacity to possess knowledge of himself and of his relationship to others in the world. It concerns his ability to identify the turbulent areas in his life and the meaning therein. Regression therapy meets the needs of the patient at the point of his life experience that will guide important decisions about his wellbeing. It does so by facilitating his understanding of the vocabulary of his experience and life stories.

Stories are the fundamental units of human experience. They function as joints that articulate the mind with the body. In the trance state, forgotten stories that constitute the patient's selfhood select themselves to manifest at the conscious level. These self-narratives surface as part of a sea of language within which we are all born as human beings. The patient's place in the social world among family members, friends and colleagues is secured by his ability to express and to understand the deeper meaning of the stories that bind him in communion with others. Through the language of the patient's life stories, regression therapy gets to the heart of his illness, and offers corrective changes that can sometimes be transformational.

Regression as a Holistic Approach

Much of the current attitude of conventional Medicine towards regression therapy is rooted in the precepts of Classical Science. In the seventeenth century Rene Descartes divided everything in the universe into two realms: (1) the realm of matter or things extended in space, known as *res extensa,* and (2) a realm of the mind known as *res cogitans.* He viewed mental and emotional content as being incapable of scientific description because they lacked physical extensions that could be quantified. Since then, all respectable knowledge of the universe was restricted to studying only those aspects that are measurable, that is, the *res extensa.* The worldview of the universe was that everything in nature could be explained in terms of interactions of matter particles. In this view, materialism constitutes the only reality. Consciousness is considered a by-product of the physical activity of the brain and matter is unconscious. The mind is inside the head and is considered only an activity of the brain. Memories are stored as material traces in the brain and assumed to be wiped out at death.

Under these precepts, mechanistic medicine is considered as the only kind that will really work. For anything to be considered real, and knowledge regarded as trustworthy, there must be measurable and reproducible parameters. When applied to healthcare, this worldview has two implications. Firstly, the inner world of emotions will not be valued in terms of having real influence on physical wellbeing, because emotions are not quantifiable. Secondly, the physical world will be considered the most important dimension in terms of exerting the strongest healing influence on the human body. At odds with this view, regression therapy works on the premise that emotional disturbances are at the root of a patient's illness, and precedes the disturbance in physiological homeostasis. It propounds the need to simultaneously treat the emotions, mind and spirit, in addition to the body, in order for the individual to self-adjust. This "holistic" approach respects the human individual for his capacity to heal himself, and regards the patient as an active partner rather than a passive recipient of care.

Conventional Medicine perceives illness as a random event, and that the latter exerts its impact on the patient "from without." For example, we think in terms of a person "catching a cold", being "hit by a heart attack" or "struck by cancer". This gives the sense that all disease causation comes from a world outside the human body. In many ways, disease is deemed as an external invader that attacks a previously healthy body. Building on this idea, curative action will logically also come from an external source. Hence, the physician will prescribe an antibiotic to inactivate a bacterium, a blood-thinner to reduce risk of vascular occlusion or a course of radiation to kill off actively growing cancer cells.

In contrast, regression therapy works "from within" the individual. It is based on the principle that the patient's body reflects the deeper struggles of his entire life. Hence, illness is deemed not to occur randomly, but when emotional, psychological or spiritual stresses have overwhelmed or weakened the body defenses. The therapeutic objective is to assist him to regain a healthy balance. Once balance is restored, his innate healing powers are activated to overcome the infection, environmental stress or cancer growth. This therapy assumes that the patient's subjective experience of his illness is paramount. It focuses on the imbalance within the individual or between the individual and other people. The physical symptoms are not ignored, but are seen as conveying a particular symbolic meaning that can be used to guide the patient to understand why the illness occurred.

As such, illness functions as a bodily message of an underlying imbalance, and is perceived as an opportunity for the individual's emotional and spiritual growth. The reason for the occurrence of an illness is interpreted in the light of something in the patient's life that needs to be changed. This may involve examining the patient's work situation, family relationships, lifestyle, exercise, rest patterns, nutrition and life purpose. The patient needs to ask why he has become sick at that particular time, and allow the illness to motivate him towards better self-awareness and self-understanding.

As doctors, many of us may have difficulty accepting that thoughts, emotions and imagination actually have healing power. While the regression therapist teaches his patient that he creates his own reality through his attitudes, emotions and beliefs, physicians on the other hand are generally unconvinced that thoughts are powerful enough to influence a person's physical reality. They are also unable to conceive how the individual's search for meaning, purpose and fulfillment can impact on physical health, even though the process comes sharply into focus during times of crisis or major illness.

"Absence of evidence is not evidence of absence."

Carl Sagan

Holistic health teaches that the root of spiritual stress often revolves around the fear of loss of life, health, love or money. This fear in turn leads to anger, guilt, depression and anxiety. Spiritual deficits leading to illness are often characterized by a lack of forgiveness, tolerance, love, wisdom, hope, courage and compassion. In regression therapy, we adopt the view that physical health begins with a conscious determination to express the goal of eliminating these fears.

The dynamics of the patient-doctor relationship is currently changing. The growth of self-responsibility and personal empowerment are two changes that our patients perceive as having a major impact on their health and wellbeing. Rather than holding the doctor responsible for the quality of their health, patients are increasingly recognizing that the ownership for eliminating their inner stresses rightfully belongs to themselves. This evolution is in the favor of the future growth of regression therapy.

Most regression therapists have observed that one fundamental change that often emerges from the patient after a successful course of therapy is his new aim to be more in touch with the divine element within himself. For the patient who has been exposed to the full range of his past life emotions during therapy sessions, he appreciates that the series of past lives are being undertaken within an environment of increasing personal responsibility and free will. As his physical symptoms vanish and emotional issues resolve with the treatment, he starts to listen to the urging of his inner voice. This leads him to the closer creation of his own reality. Despite his setbacks, he may be observed to have acquired remarkable motivation to move on in life.

Scientific Validation

Reincarnation is not an article of faith, but a theory offered to explain certain phenomena and observations in our lives. We grow up under the influence of materialistic theory, which assumes that memory is somehow stored only at the physical level, and there is no other way of storing it. This doctrinal bias hinders us from going beyond conventional scientific thinking to understand the profound mysteries of the material universe, including past life memory.

During the scientific revolution of the seventeenth century, Descartes viewed the world as consisting of *res extensa*, the set of extended things or the material realm which is objective, and *res cogitans*, the set of thinking things or the realm of the mind which does not have a proper existence in time and space.

The concept of reincarnation is foundational to past life regression therapy. It may be defined as the re-embodiment of an immaterial part of an individual, or his soul consciousness after death, into a new body. From there, it proceeds to lead a new life unconscious of its past experiences, but carrying its existential essence from previous lives. The body, which is the material part, falls within the realm of *res extensa*, whereas the immaterial part, which has not been studied by scientists, falls within the realm of *res cogitans*.

With the advent of modern science, the two realms, *res extensa* and *res cogitans,* are being merged. We now understand that the universe cannot be broken up into two independent arbitrary realms and studied independently. Researchers have since begun to examine the concept of reincarnation scientifically.

The current paradigm of the universe is one that sprang out of nothingness 13.7 billion years ago in an event named as the Big Bang. It is viewed as a lifeless collection of particles bouncing against each other and obeying predetermined rules. The model is somewhat akin to that of a watch that has somehow wound itself, and now is allowing itself to unwind in a rather random and semi-predictable manner. However, human consciousness, a critical component of the universe, has been left out of the model. Dr. Robert Lanza, who has been on the frontier of cloning and stem cell research, has recently proposed in his theory of Biocentrism[37] that human consciousness has created the universe and not the other way round. To understand the nature of the universe, its origin and parameters would require an understanding of how the observer and his consciousness play a role.

As a term, consciousness is hard to define. It is often used synonymously with "awareness" and encompasses experience, thoughts, feelings, images, dreams, body sensations, and so on. It is commonly used to refer to a state of "wakefulness", or used to mean "knowledge" in the sense that if one is conscious of something, one also has knowledge of it.

---

[37] "Biocentrism: How Life created the Universe" by Robert Lanza.
http://www.robertlanzabiocentrism.com/msnbc-publishes-free-online-abridgment-of-biocentrism/

"The history of Science is not a mere record of isolated discoveries; it is a narrative of the conflict of two contending powers, the expansive force of the human intellect on one side, and the compression arising from traditional faith and human interests on the other."

John William Draper, M.D.

In: History of the Conflict Between
Religion and Science, 1881

The belief that man is more than a material body goes beyond the twilight of recorded history. According to Plato, the material body interacts with the soul of the individual. In acquiring knowledge, the body influences the soul through the operation of its senses, but the soul provides the person with the means of understanding the true nature of the world. The soul is the knowing agent; it enables the body to move and act and is the source of reason and consciousness.

The notion of consciousness lies at the heart of the theory of reincarnation. The latter could be tested by the scientific method as expounded by Richard Feynman, Nobel Laureate in Physics, in his 1964 lecture. The process has three steps: *theorize, observe* and *confirm* (Fig. 5).

(1) In the first step, a new theory is formulated after studying the relevant phenomenon. As reincarnation is a very old and ancient theory with a big fraction of the world population believing in it, this step has long been completed.

(2) The second step involves asking ourselves: "If the idea is correct, what would we expect to observe?" In other words, the theory is now used to predict observations that one should be able

to make, if the theory is correct. For this step, a large amount of data and information have already been gathered. They are from three main sources: (i) people, especially children, who remember their past lives; (ii) people who are able to recall their past lives under hypnotic regression; and (iii) child prodigies who can make use of knowledge and experience gathered in past lives.

Fig. 5: Scientific Theory Testing and Knowledge Building

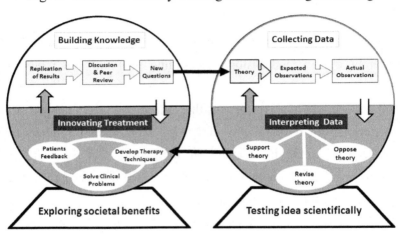

(3) The third step involves examining these observations to see if they are agreeable with the predictions. When actual observations match expected observations, the theory is considered acceptable. Dr. Ian Stevenson (1918–2007), a psychiatrist from the University of Virginia School of Medicine, devoted his life to the scientific documentation of past life memories of children from all over the world. All his observations are in agreement with step 2 of the scientific process and match what we would expect from the reincarnation theory. He captured over 3000 cases in his file and to date has provided

the best evidence yet for reincarnation.[38] This successfully completes the test for scientific validity of the theory of reincarnation.

Building the knowledge base in a scientific fashion involves a second layer in the schema (Fig. 5). The real test for the usefulness of any theory lies in what happens when one applies it. Knowledge fuels technology development. Likewise, the idea of reincarnation has fuelled the innovation of regression techniques which, when applied to the treatment of clinical problems, has led to distinct, observable and positive outcomes that are consistent and reproducible. The sharing of clinical experiences and data through discussion, publication and peer review excites the asking of probing questions. Questions in turn pave the way for medical researchers to refine the theory, and enter into further cycles of idea testing.

> *"Materialists deny anything that is beyond the physical, hence, even the possibility of reincarnation. Fundamentalists repudiate reincarnation because they automatically reject anything that is not part of their dogma. Skeptics do so because they enjoy ridiculing everything they haven't personally experienced."*
>
> Dr. Robert Leichtman, M.D.
> In: 'From Heaven to Earth' series

---

[38] "Twenty Cases Suggestive of Reincarnation", 2nd ed. The University Press of Virginia, 1974, *European Cases of the Reincarnation Type*, MacFarland & Co. Inc, 2003

However, we are aware that there is a social perspective to Science. In his book, *The Structure of Scientific Revolutions*[39], Thomas Kuhn pointed out that Science is a collective activity and scientists are therefore subject to all the usual constraints of social life. This includes peer pressure and the need to conform to group norms. When the group norm is to hold on to the centuries-old assumption of materialism that has hardened into dogma, scientists will continue to adopt the worldview that materialism is the one and only reality. The concept of consciousness will therefore continue to be relegated to the physical domain of brain activity. From this standpoint, it can be appreciated why the idea of a human being as having a material body plus an immaterial part (consciousness) that enters into a scientifically unknown state and reappears after a period of time, continues to invite resistance.

Currently, the major arguments put forth by critics against past life memories rest on two main fronts:

1. Prompting – It is argued that the reported cases of past life memory occurred in people who were already believers in reincarnation. So, if a child appeared to be referring to a past life, his parents would have encouraged him and unwittingly fed him with information about a deceased person of whom the child believed that he was a reincarnate. Though plausible, this is unlikely to be an adequate explanation. This is because the belief in reincarnation was rare in Western countries in the earlier decades when the data of the reported cases were collected. Hence, any children who mentioned something

---

[39] *The Structure of Scientific Revolutions*, University of Chicago Press, 4th Ed 2012.

about past lives or hinted at it would likely have been ignored, silenced or even scoffed at.

2. Cryptamnesia – Cryptamnesia is the conscious appearance in an individual of memory images that are not recognized as such but as original creations. It is often argued that a child who recalled past life memories could have previously obtained the same information from another source but had forgotten about it. This source could be a book, magazine, newspaper article, television or an overheard conversation. This is a possibility but it is not a satisfactory explanation for long-distance cases. When the past life had occurred in a geographically distant locality, too much detailed information would be needed by the child to put together a believable set of past life memories in such a situation. Woolger estimated that, in his personal experience, cryptamnesia formed only about 2 to 3 percent of his patients who recalled their past lives.[40]

Philosophical Discourse

One of the natural laws of the universe is the law of periodicity, and this governs all manifestations of living and non-living things. Periodicity refers to the state of being regularly repeating. The night follows the day in a twenty-four-hour cycle and the four seasons follow one another in a rhythmic sequence, year after year. The body, too, has its biological cycles where periods of activity follow periods of rest. In the heart cycle, the diastole

---

[40] "Are Past Lives real? Could they be important for our health and well-being today?"
http://www.superconsciousness.com/topics/knowledge/are-past-lives-real-could-they-be-important-our-health-and-well-being-today

follows the systole. In the brain, periods of wakefulness alternate with periods of sleepiness. Psychologically, cycles of depression are followed by periods of exhilaration.

In the larger scheme of things, life itself can be seen to unfold itself through a series of rhythmic and recurring patterns. The Self expresses itself in thought, desire and action in its arena of existence. However, during its period of rest and revitalization, the Self reviews its experiences of existence and shapes them into new capabilities and powers for its next cycle of activity. These alternating periods of rest and action of the immortal Self is the basis of the philosophical framework of reincarnation.

Reincarnation may be viewed as a method of transportation in our evolutionary journey as humans, in which one can choose one's rate of progress. The choice can be based on our thoughts, desires, actions or our accumulated capacities. In this perspective, reincarnation is considered an opportunity for each of us to travel on our journey of life according to our uniqueness, to realize our chosen spiritual goal. On the other hand, reincarnation may also be perceived as a tool that life uses to gain experience for the Self to learn how to live.

Fundamentally in reincarnation, the conscious self (or soul) exists before birth and continues its journey after death. It is continually growing and is treading its way from an awakened state towards one of splendid maturity. It thirsts for the experiences that will make it a perfect being. At each stage of its evolutionary journey, it gathers around itself an appropriate mental and emotional field and fashions a physical vehicle according to the laws of heredity. As it moves through its cycle of birth, maturity, old age and death it learns its lesson, while allowing death to set aside a rest period for it to assimilate its experiences into a more mature wisdom. With the latter, the soul may begin another incarnation.

A question that is commonly asked is: "If I have past lives, why do I not remember them?" However, few of us highlight the fact that we also forget a significant part of our present lives. For instance, most of us cannot remember learning how to walk, but the fact that we can walk is proof that we did learn. If our memory is so distracted by the experiences in our body in the present life, how much more would we be affected by the numerous past experiences in our former lives? Yet, the amazing truth is that our past life memories do not disappear altogether; they remain accessible with the aid of a regression therapist.

The great lesson of reincarnation is that our powers are infinite; our opportunities are eternal and our goals divine. There is no goal so high that we cannot reach it through our persistent effort, although several lifetimes may be necessary. Opportunities return to us life after life. To live in awareness of this universal cycle of rhythmic change is to be free from fear and doubt. Regressing a patient back to his past lives therefore helps to free him from the prison of his temporary personality into a nobler realization of his eternal purpose. It affirms that life is meaningful and that all suffering has its significance. In the light of reincarnation, he may then be able to perceive every moment of his current life as a doorway to the Immortal. Birth, suffering and death are only milestones along the way.

Further Reading

Bennet, G., *The Wound and the Doctor: Healing, Technology and Power in Modern Medicine,* **Secker & Warburg 1987** – This interesting book is written by a doctor who started his career as a surgeon and went on to become a psychotherapist and psychiatrist. He addresses the issue of why many doctors are unhappy with the work they do and many patients are unhappy about the care they receive, and how things could be better. He also dwells on the role of complementary therapies.

Churchill, R., *Regression Hypnotherapy – Transcripts of Transformation,* **Transforming Press, 2002** – This book contains teaching material and full transcripts of current life regression sessions for a variety of conditions including phobias, grief, lack of confidence, sabotaging success, unhealthy relationships, abuse and fear of abandonment. It is an excellent guide for beginners, as well as a useful reference for experienced therapists.

TenDam, H., *Deep Healing,* **Tasso, 1996** (order from Hans' email; tasso@damconsult.nl.). Regression therapy techniques used by Hans TenDam, who is one of the pioneers in regression therapy.

LaBay, M.L., *Past Life Regression: A Guide for Practitioners,* **Trafford Publishing, 2004** – A light reading book on the practice of past life therapy that incorporates stories from the author's personal experience. The author blends hypnotherapy techniques with philosophy, intuition and reincarnation theory to catalyze growth and transformation in her clients.

Lucas, W.B., *Regression Therapy: A Handbook for Professionals, Vols I & II,* **Book Solid Press, 1992** – The two volumes are a classic for regression therapists. It is a multi-author work on regression therapy compiled by a professional psychologist and Jungian analyst. Volume I focuses on past life therapy while Volume II touches on prenatal and birth experiences, childhood traumas and death.

Tomlinson, A., *Healing the Eternal Soul,* **From the Heart Press, 2012** – This is a definitive reference work in regression therapy. The author shares his valuable experience in detail and uses concrete case studies to illustrate his points and techniques. It is a captivating book and a must-have for all students of regression therapy.

Tomlinson, A. (ed.), *Transforming the Eternal Soul,* **From the Heart Press, 2011** – Written as a follow-on from *Healing the Eternal Soul,* this book is packed with illuminating case studies and specialized therapy techniques. The chapters include: empowering a client; working with difficult clients; spiritual inner child regression; clearing energy; crystal therapy in regression; spiritual emergency; and integrating therapy into a client's current life.

Woolger, R.J., *Healing Your Past Lives,* **Sounds True Inc., 2004** – This short book provides a series of interesting case studies that illustrate the power of uncovering past lives in the healing process. It gives insight as to how current life symptoms could be related to past life dramas and frozen memories. It also provides the reader with the key to unlocking the mysteries and questions they struggle with in their current lives.

Woolger, R.J., *Other Lives, Other Selves – A Jungian Psychotherapist Discovers Past Lives,* **Bantam Books, 1988.** This is a fascinating book that presents the author's original insights into the emerging psychology of reincarnation. The book draws on both Western science and Eastern spirituality and explains how past lives may form the basis of transformation and healing in our lives.

Regression Therapy Associations

Society for Medical Advance and Research in Regression Therapy (SMAR-RT)

This international society, formed in April 2013, aims to conduct and coordinate research in regression therapy. It is led by medical doctors who share the vision to bring about the integration of complementary and holistic approaches into conventional Medicine. It is a non-profit organization and hopes to raise awareness of the effectiveness of regression therapy as a healing tool within the medical profession.

Website: http://www.smar-rt.org

Earth Association of Regression Therapy (EARTh)

This is an independent association with the objective to create and maintain an international standard in regression therapy and improve and enlarge its professional acceptance. Every summer it offers a series of workshops for ongoing professional development. It aims to advance the field by providing a meeting ground for regression therapists through conferences and meetings.

Website: http://www.earth-association.org

Spiritual Regression Therapy Association (SRTA)

This is an international association of regression therapists that respect the spiritual nature of their clients. Established by Andy Tomlinson, they are trained by the *Past Life Regression Academy* to Earth professional standards. The association provides networking, professional ongoing development and the promotion of regression therapy.

Website: http://www.regressionassociation.com

Association for Regression and Reincarnation Research (ARRR)

This association was founded by Dr. Newton Kondaveti and launched in Hyderabad, India, in 2010 with the aim to promote research in regression and reincarnation, and work towards increasing awareness and acceptance of past life therapy among people in India and all over the world. It publishes a newsletter, a magazine, holds annual conventions and conducts certification examinations for professionals practicing past life regression therapy.

Website: http://www.arrrglobal.org

International Board of Regression Therapy (IBRT)

This is an independent examining and certifying board for past life therapists, researchers and training programs. Its mission is to set professional standards for regression therapists and organizations. The website has a list of international accredited past life and regression therapy training organizations.

Website: http://www.ibrt.org.

Healing Deep Hurt Within

Author: Dr. Peter Mack

from the heart press

(Swedish and French editions available)

This book is based on a true story of an emotionally traumatized lady who suffered from unexplained syncope, dissociative amnesia, insomnia, auditory hallucinations and suicidal tendencies. She recovered from her devastated state after intensive regression therapy over an 18-day period. She underwent transformational healing and moved on in life. Upon recovery, she requested that her physician-therapist write up the story of her healing journey.

"A book that touches my heart." – Rudy Phen, Physician

"I couldn't put the book down, and finished reading it in three hours. It has been almost a week, and I can still feel the effect." – Swan Ang, Management Trainer

"The drama is overwhelming. There is a sense of liberation after reading it." – Leong Saw Wei, Managing Director

"This book is a must read for those who are ready to assume responsibility and live their life to the fullest." – Theresa Chee, Life Coach and Educational Consultant

Life-Changing Moments in Inner Healing

Author: Dr. Peter Mack

This book contains the regression stories of four patients who went through past life healing. The first patient experiences unexplained visions of an unidentified lady and phobia of water. The second patient is faced with serious problems of procrastination and anger management since childhood. The third patient has problems of memory loss, and fear of success and public speaking. The fourth patient is afflicted with an irrational fear of snakes. All four patients went through transformational healing after regression therapy.

"I read this amazing book in one sitting and just couldn't put it down." – Rosa Lilia Castillo Maya, Housewife

"An awesome book with many interesting and fascinating past life stories." – Wendy Yeung, Holistic Therapist

"A highly recommended book for those seeking alternative healing therapies." – Joyce Cheng, Neurofeedback Therapist

"This book joins a deserving place alongside Dr Weis book on my bookshelf." – Tan Cheen Chong, Technol Marketing Specialist

ss'
ogy

270

CPSIA information can be obtained at www.ICGtesting.com
Printed in the USA
BVOW11s1534071215

429599BV00011B/103/P